Sam—Sam Spade is Dashiel Hammett's rough-and-ready private eye, introduced in *The Maltese Falcon* (1930) . . .

Zenobia—Once the defiant, powerful, and ambitious queen of Palmyra, east of Syria, she takes on a new identity in Nathaniel Hawthorne's *The Blithedale Romance* (1852) . . .

Gawain—Loyal, courteous, and bursting with honor, he is the hero of *Sir Gawain and the Green Knight* (Arthurian legend of the late-fourteenth century) and appears in Sir Thomas Malory's *Le Morte d'Arthur* (1469). Among his noble deeds, he somehow manages to resist the amorous entreaties of King Bercilak's wanton wife . . .

From the work of the world's greatest authors comes this collection of names for your baby, ranging from the widely popular to the highly uncommon—names that celebrate your traditions and tastes, honor your favorite books, and promise a wonderful answer for the day your child asks: *Where did my name come from?* . . .

THE *Literary Baby* NAME BOOK

Names Inspired by the World's Most Beloved Books, Poems, and Stories

THE LITERARY BABY NAME BOOK

*Names Inspired by the World's Most Beloved
Books, Poems, and Stories*

Tershia d'Elgin

B
BERKLEY BOOKS, NEW YORK

THE LITERARY BABY NAME BOOK

A Berkley Book / published by arrangement with
the author

PRINTING HISTORY
Berkley edition / November 2001

All rights reserved.
Copyright © 2001 by Tershia d'Elgin
Book design by Kristin del Rosario
Cover design by Erika Fusari
Cover photograph by Elizabeth Hathon
This book, or parts thereof, may not be reproduced in
any form without permission.
For information address:
The Berkley Publishing Group, a division of Penguin Putnam Inc.,
375 Hudson Street, New York, New York 10014.

Visit our website at
www.penguinputnam.com

ISBN: 0-425-18220-7

BERKLEY®
Berkley Books are published by The Berkley Publishing Group,
a division of Penguin Putnam Inc., 375 Hudson Street,
New York, New York 10014.
BERKLEY and the "B" design
are trademarks belonging to Penguin Putnam Inc.

PRINTED IN THE UNITED STATES OF AMERICA

10 9 8 7 6 5 4 3 2 1

To dear Wilma Buchman,
my mentor in all matters literary

$\mathscr{C}$ONTENTS

INTRODUCTION

*J*UST as we parents do, writers give birth and name their literary offspring. They nurse their characters through trials and triumphs, both commonplace and fantastic. Growing before our eyes on every page, the characters come alive. And their names do, too, even later, after the books are closed. Every time we hear names like Scarlett and Heathcliff and Juliet and Hercules, great stories replay in our heads. A tradition this rich deserves to multiply, I think. Therefore, my book goes so far as to propose that expectant parents incarnate these heroes and heroines, right in their own families!

For me, compiling these names was a wondrous excursion through centuries' worth of creativity. Time and again, I remarked on the immortality of characters that sprang from writers' imaginations. My intent was to compile a fair representation of literature's immortal greats, and then, less objectively, of the characters that had special meaning to me. I soon realized that to do justice to this project would take not months, but a lifetime, and so I apologize. Unfortunately, not every name, not even every important work, is represented here. I wish it were. Though it is not comprehensive, this compilation needed to be completed . . . because soon-to-be babies await their literary names.

Here I share reminders of writing that brought Clorinda, Tancred, Endymion, Della, and Atticus to life. As you search for a baby name among these pages, you'll find Helen, Alexander, Hester, and Gregor. Please remember, as I did in compiling the list, that wholly sympathetic and even heroic literary characters, like flesh and blood, are never entirely free of foibles. In fact, it is their shortcomings that hasten the plot along and make them lovable. So, expectant mothers and fathers should not be surprised by duality in a name, as in a child. It seems to be what makes us human. Or as the poet William Blake wrote in *The Marriage of Heaven and Hell* (1790),

> *Without contraries is no progression. Attraction and repulsion, reason and energy, love and hate, are necessary to human existence.*

My appreciation for the attraction of opposites and, more importantly, for the *beauty* of opposites, was not fully formed before I myself gave birth to a child. But it must have lurked subconsciously, because we named our son Diego after a literary superhero with a double identity, Diego de la Vega. In 1919, Johnston McCulley created the retiring Spanish don and his more aggressive alter ego, Zorro, who corrected the ills of villainous early Californian autocrats. Our literary baby name worked! From the beginning, our child Diego has had a keen compassion for the underdog. Eleven years later and he still loves his name.

Inspired by this personal success and the love Diego has brought me, I offer you this book. It revisits a thousand characters and their personalities. I haven't done all the work for you, though. When you find a name that appeals to you, have a look at the novel, drama, or poem itself. You might want to learn more about the character you'll be using as a namesake. Just to be certain, why not wait to name your baby, as the Native Americans did, until the child is born? Then decide.

I listed each name under the section in which it first appears in my resources. Believing that readers will want to discover other characters of that name, I cite subsequent usage there. Thus, you will find the similarities and discrepancies that different authors attributed to each name.

I hope that reintroducing these great characters will enrich the spectrum of forenames out there in the world. When we hear the names, it will pay tribute to the magnificent minds that gladdened our lives with literature. May children flaunt their literary heritage, and in good spirit!

THE OLDEST NAMES:

Ancient Names (from Sumeria through the Roman Empire)

❧ ❧

*Y*OU'LL find names from these many centuries ago are like charmed threads. Following them leads to the very foundations of civilization. The ancient world spawned some of the most sensational epic poetry and ballads of all time. Explaining the natural world and concerned with love, wars, and rites, these classic works sowed a crop of characters and events that subsequent writers frequently harvested. For centuries to come, poems, dramas, and books recapitulated the stories, and often improved on them, adding depth and lyricism to the names themselves.

Ancient Women's Names

Andromache—Andromache is Hector's long-suffering wife and then widow in Homer's *The Iliad* and *The Odyssey* (ninth century B.C.), Euripides'

The Trojan Women and *Andromache* (fifth century B.C.), William Shakespeare's *Troilus and Cressida* (1602), and Jean Racine's play *Andromaque* (1667).

Antigone—Oedipus' dutiful, noble, and brave daughter, Antigone, acts as his guide after he blinds himself. After burying her brothers, who die in battle, she is condemned to be buried alive by Creon, the father of her lover, Haemon. When she preempts this by hanging herself, Haemon kills himself, according to *Antigone* as told by Sophocles in the fifth century B.C. and several other writers including Jean Anouilh in his play *Antigone* (1942), which satirizes the French government.

Aphrodite—Aphrodite is the Greek goddess of love, exalted by Sappho, the greatest female poet of ancient Greece, in the "Ode to Aphrodite" of around 600 B.C.

Artemis—Artemis, the headstrong goddess of the hunt, champions family planning by demanding chastity in her minions and protecting childbirth. She figures prominently in Euripides' work of the fifth century B.C., *Iphigenia in Aulis* and *Hippolytus*.

Atalanta—According to Ovid's *Metamorphoses* (first century A.D.), Atalanta is the proud huntress, so fleet she will only dally for enchanted golden apples dropped by Melanion, or in some versions, Hippomenes. Find her again in William Morris's *Earthly Paradise* (1868) and Algernon Charles Swinburne's *Atalanta in Calydon* (1865).

Calypso—Calypso, an island nymph, clingingly detains Odysseus, though she eventually helps him depart in Homer's *The Iliad* and *The Odyssey* (ninth century B.C.).

Cassandra—This Trojan princess has the gift of prophecy, given to her by Apollo, her lover. Agamemnon captures Cassandra to make her his slave and mistress in *Agamemnon* by Aeschylus (sixth century B.C.).

Chloë—Chloë, a rustic maiden with artistic flair, is in love with Daphnis in *Daphnis and Chloë,* by the Greek poet Longus of the classical era.

Chryseis—Chryseis is Chryses' alluring daughter, taken captive during the Trojan War by Agamemnon, on whom her father rained a plague according to Homer's *The Iliad* and *The Odyssey* (ninth century B.C.).

Circe—Circe is a paranoid enchantress who turns men into pigs (not as easy as it sounds), in Homer's *The Iliad* and *The Odyssey* (ninth century B.C.).

Clytemnestra—Agamemnon's inconstant wife has an affair with Aegisthus while Agamemnon is away.

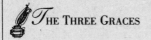

THE THREE GRACES

Euphrosyne (Joy)
Aglaia (Brilliance)
Thalia (the Flowering)

Though a sympathetic character in *The Oresteia* by
Aeschylus (sixth century B.C.), Clytemnestra is nevertheless ruthless, stubborn, and vindictive—not unlike a lot of women; however, she carries her
feelings to an extreme: She murders her husband.
In retribution, her son Orestes snuffs out Aegisthus
and subsequently murders her. In William Faulkner's *Absalom, Absalom!* (1936), she is a servile
character at beck and call until her arsonous death,
along with Henry Sutpen.

Criseyde—Also known as Cressida, she is the daughter of the Trojan soothsayer Calchas. She vows eternal love to Troilus, but during the siege of Troy,
she betrays him. Homer, Geoffrey Chaucer, and
William Shakespeare retold this story.

Delia—Delia is a sweet and inviting shepherdess in
Virgil's *Bucolics* of the first century A.D.

Delilah—Sort of a perfidious vixen, Delilah is Sam-
son's lover and hairdresser in the Old Testament.

Dido—Dido, the queen of Carthage in Virgil's first-
century epic, *The Aeneid*, though lovely and regal,
demonstrates more romantic passion than inner resources, because she commits suicide when Aeneas
leaves. Christopher Marlowe, too, wrote about her
fate in *The Tragedy of Dido* (1593).

Electra—After Electra's mother, Clytemnestra, kills
Electra's unfortunate father, Agamemnon, Electra's
unresolved libidinous feelings for Agamemnon
prompt her to convince her brother Orestes to mur-

der Clytemnestra and her mother's lover—an early example of pathological behavior in *The Oresteia* by Aeschylus (sixth century B.C.).

Europa—Europa is the famous lovely who swam with a white bull in Homer's *The Iliad* and *The Odyssey* (ninth century B.C.).

Eurydice—This hell-bound beauty is a dryad beloved by Orpheus in Ovid's *Metamorphoses* (first century A.D.), Claudio Monteverdi's *Orfeo* (1607), Franz Joseph Haydn's *Orfeo* (1805), Christoph Gluck's *Orpheus and Eurydice* (1762), and Jean Cocteau's *Orfée* (1950).

Eve—Not only the overly curious gobbler of the forbidden fruit, Eve is also the mother of the rest of us.

Galatea—Intriguing to all who feel they could craft their own mate, Galatea first appears in Ovid's *Metamorphoses* (first century A.D.). She is a statue of Aphrodite that comes to life at the request of her sculptor, Pygmalion. The story is often retold, notably in W. S. Gilbert's *Pygmalion and Galatea* (1871) and George Bernard Shaw's *Pygmalion* (1913).

Helen—The story of the most exquisite woman of her time well illustrates the burden of beauty. Her abduction from Sparta by Paris topples Troy, maiming or killing nearly everyone in the telling, by Homer in *The Iliad* and *The Odyssey* (ninth century B.C.). Euripides, in his fifth-century play *The Trojan*

Women, and many writers since have revisited the sorry scene, including Dante Gabriel Rossetti, in a poem, "Troy Town" (1870). Johann Wolfgang von Goethe had Faust fall in love with Helen and attempt her abduction from Paris in *Faust* (1808).

Hermione—Hermione is the passionate and possessive daughter of Helen and Menelaus in Homer's ninth-century *The Iliad* and *The Odyssey*, Euripides' *Trojan Women* and *Andromache* (fifth century B.C.), William Shakespeare's *Troilus and Cressida* (1602), and Jean Racine's *Andromaque* (1667). Later, Hermione is Leontes' unjustly accused wife who disappears from him only to reappear as a statue that comes to life in William Shakespeare's *Winter's Tale* (1611). Hermione is also Harry Potter's young witch friend in the recent *Harry Potter* series (1999) by J. K. Rowling.

Hippolyta—The queen of the Amazons and Theseus' sporty warrior wife fights and dies at his side. She is a happy spouse in William Shakespeare's *A Midsummer Night's Dream* (1595).

Iphigenia—When one needs a fair wind to speed Greek ships to Troy, who better to sacrifice than Electra and Orestes' sister? At the last minute Iphigenia is saved by Artemis, whose priestess she becomes. She is a favorite of the Greek tragedian Euripides, who wrote two plays about her in the fifth century B.C. Walter Savage Landor also wrote a poem about her, "Iphigenia" (1846).

Ishtar—Ishtar, who is also called Inanna, is the Babylonian goddess of love and war, an unusual but apt combination of responsibilities in which "all is fair." She appears in *The Epic of Gilgamesh* (2000 B.C.).

Isis—The Greeks and Romans carried Egypt's most important goddess, Isis, forward in time. Roman satirist Lucius Apuleius wrote about her as "the universal mother of nature" in *The Golden Ass* (second century A.D.). Edmund Spenser used Isis and Osiris as metaphors for English equity and justice in *The Faerie Queen* (1590–96), and John Milton nestled Isis among his fallen angels in *Paradise Lost* (1667). The idiom "lifting the veil of Isis" means uncovering a great mystery.

Ismene—Ismene, Antigone's timid sister, has sibling devotions that go over the top. She requests to be buried alive like her sister in Sophocles' fifth-century B.C. *Antigone*.

Ki—Ki is the Sumerian earth goddess in mythology translated from cuneiform.

Laïs—Laïs was the most exquisite woman of Corinth, a hetaera (courtesan) of the fourth century B.C. The jealous women of Corinth mangled her with their bobkins.

Lavinia—In *The Aeneid*, first-century poet Virgil described how Aeneas kills the Rutulian king Turnus in a war for the fair hand of Lavinia, the princess of Latium. In William Shakespeare's *Titus Andronicus* of 1590, a lamentable Lavinia, Titus's only daughter, is raped, has her hands and tongue cut off, and is in the end put out of her misery by Titus.

Lysistrata—Lysistrata is the heroine of a comedy of the same name by Aristophanes, sort of a fifth-century suffragette who influences Greek wives into taking oaths of celibacy until they get their own way.

Medea—Medea, a hyperpassionate enchantress, helps her husband, Jason, secure his fleece. When he opts out of the relationship, she takes revenge by killing their children (not necessarily an option to encourage in your own daughter), in Apollonius of Rhodes' *Argonautica* (third century B.C.), Euripides' play *Medea* (fifth century B.C.), and Robinson Jeffers's *Medea* (1946).

Omphale—The Lydian queen Omphale is Hercules' lover. Beguiling in pelts, she trades clothes with him according to Ovid's *Metamorphoses* (first century A.D.).

Penelope—Penelope is Odysseus' long-awaiting and ingenious wife who knows the difference between warp and weft, as described by Homer in *The Iliad* and *The Odyssey* (ninth century B.C.).

Penthesilea—Penthesilea is a beautiful, courageous queen of the Amazons, slain, regrettably, by Achilles according to Homer in *The Iliad* and *The Odyssey* (ninth century B.C.). Heinrich von Kleist retells the story in *Penthesilea and Achilles* (1808).

Phyrne—Phyrne, like Laïs, was a fourth-century courtesan or hetaera, but in Athens rather than Corinth. She lent her accumulated wealth to the city's building projects.

Thetis—The Greek sea goddess Thetis is Achilles' mother. Her plea to the gods to avenge her son set off many of the tragedies of Homer's *The Iliad* and *The Odyssey* (ninth century B.C.).

Virginia—The story of an exquisite young plebeian killed by her father before she could become Appius Claudius Crassus's slave is relayed by Roman historian Livy in his *History of Rome* (9 B.C.), as well as by Francesco Petrarch in *Virginia* and Geoffrey Chaucer in *The Canterbury Tales* in the fourteenth century. The Virginia in Bernardin de Saint-Pierre's *Paul and Virginia* (1787) is Paul's soul mate; they are raised together to die within sight of each other in Mauritius. "Virginia" is the recipient of a letter from the editor of the *New York Sun,* 1897, in the famous "Yes, Virginia, there is a Santa Claus." Virginia Carvel is the southerner to Stephen Brice's Yankee in Winston Churchill's novel *The Crisis* (1901).

Ancient Men's Names

Aaron—Moses' brother and right-hand man, as well as the original priest, is punished for his lack of faith in the Old Testament. Aron Trask is Caleb's winning but willful brother in John Steinbeck's *East of Eden* (1952).

Achilles—Achilles is one of the most complex characters of ancient times—fleet, brave, fond of women, fierce, inconsistent, jealous, loyal, and invulnerable everywhere . . . except one small spot, according to Homer in *The Iliad* and *The Odyssey* (ninth century B.C.) and many other writers.

Achates—Achates is Aeneas' bosom buddy and henchman in Virgil's *The Aeneid* (9–19 A.D.).

Actaeon—Actaeon is a mythical voyeur who, having observed Artemis in the buff, is changed by her into a stag. His dogs then attack and tear him to bits according to Ovid's *Metamorphoses* (first century A.D.). Actaeon's plight is evoked metaphorically by Andrew Richter in *Actaeon* (1997), his story of a Jewish boy spying on a Protestant girl.

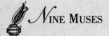 *N*INE MUSES

Calliope—epic poetry

Clio—history

Erato—love poetry

Euterpe—music

Melpomene—tragedy

Polyhymnia—hymns

Terpsichore—choral song and dance

Thalia—comedy

Urania—astronomy

Aeneas—Aeneas is the broad-shouldered adventurer who carries the plot of Virgil's great literary epic, *The Aeneid* (9–19 A.D.) on through twelve books, from the fall of Troy to Africa and back to Italy.

Agamemnon—Agamemnon is a Mycenaean king who leads the Greeks into Troy only to be murdered by his wife on his return, featured in Homer's *The Iliad* and *The Odyssey* (ninth century B.C.), *The Oresteia*, a sixth-century B.C. Greek tragedy by Aeschylus, and elsewhere.

Agathocles—Agathocles is an ambitious self-starter who rises from nothing to become the tyrant of Sicily from 361–289 B.C. His story, always called by his name, was retold by Voltaire, Richard Perrington, and Caroline Pichler.

Ajax—Ajax is the self-confident chest-beating king of Salamis whose greatness went to waste as he went mad with jealousy, according to Homer in *The Iliad* and *The Odyssey* (ninth century B.C.).

Apollo—The Greek god of light was celebrated early on by the Greek poet and musician Thaletus and again by Terpander in the seventh century B.C. Apollo, however dazzling, is often spurned in love despite his power. His insistence on justice is evident in his defense of Orestes, inacted in Aeschylus' sixth-century B.C. *Eumenides*. Friedrich Nietzsche distinguished "Apollonian" as having to do with rational thought, by contrast with "Dionysian," which is instinctive and chaotic.

Ascanius—In ancient times, and forward into the Elizabethan period, claims of Trojan heritage were as popular as "Elvis Lives" stories are today. To satisfy his patron, Augustus, Virgil made Aeneas' son Ascanius the founder of Alba Longa, mother city of Rome. All Romans thus descend from Ascanius, imparting this much-sought-after Trojan heritage.

Daphnis—Daphnis, a Sicilian shepherd, has an ambiguous romantic history. His love may be unrequited or perhaps he just refused love in *Daphnis and Chloë* by the Greek poet Longus of the classical era.

Diomedes—Caution. This trouble-causing, daring, and foolhardy warrior seduces Criseyde (Cressida) away from Troilus. Without him, Homer, Chaucer, and William Shakespeare would have lacked an edge in their stories of Troilus and Criseyde.

Ea—Ea is the Babylonian god of wisdom and the elements from *The Epic of Gilgamesh* (2000 B.C.). His responsibilities include keeping Earth and the universe beyond from catastrophe.

Gilgamesh—Gilgamesh is a tyrant king, eventually befriended by a hairy man-beast sent to settle him, Enkidu, in *The Epic of Gilgamesh* (2000 B.C.).

Hephaestus—Hephaestus is the Greek god of metalworking and fire. He forges a throne for his mother, Hera, out of which she cannot rise, according to Ovid's *Metamorphoses* (first century A.D.).

Hercules—History's most notable beefcake, Hercules is strong and determined, accomplishing twelve feats of derring-do and vanquishing the most daunting players of the ancient world. He is less well known for killing his wife and children. His accomplishments appear in Peisander of Rhodes' *Heracleia* (seventh century B.C.), Panyasis of Halicarnassus' *Heracleia*, Euripides' *Alcestis* (fifth century B.C.), Sophocles' *Trachiniai* and *Philoctetes* and *Heracles mainomenos* (fifth century B.C.), Seneca's *Hercules furens* (first century A.D.), scads of other places, and on television. A different sort of Hercules, Hercule Poirot, of Agatha Christie's invention, is a Belgian sleuth. Though small in stature, he is enormous in ability and in his own estimation. He appears in many of her detective stories in the 1920s and '30s.

Hermes—His first day on earth is busy: Hermes invents the lyre and steals Apollo's flock, as celebrated in Sophocles' play *Icheutai* (fifth century B.C.). Big and sneaky, he is worshipped as a "herm," a phallic form. A later Hermes, Hermes Trismegistus, is a mythical philosopher and magician. During the Middle Ages, his name was signed to some books on mysticism. He is mentioned in "Il Penseroso" (1632) by John Milton and is the subject of a poem by Percy Bysshe Shelley.

Hippolytus (Hippolyte)—Hippolytus is Phaedra's honorable stepson, whom she craves. When Hippolytus rejects her attentions, Phaedra attempts vengeance by falsely accusing him of raping her. His father, Theseus, outraged, enjoins Poseidon to drown poor Hippolytus. *Hippolytus* is a fifth-century B.C. tragedy by Euripides. Writer Gustave Flaubert makes Hippolyte the wretched clubfoot in his *Madame Bovary* (1856). Hippolyte's condition sets Emma's mind in action.

Ishmael—In the Old Testament, Ishmael is the son of Abraham and Hagar, a surrogate chosen when Sarah could not conceive. The name is a sort of prayer, meaning "may God hear." Ishmael, narrator in Herman Melville's *Moby-Dick* (1851), announces, "Call me Ishmael."

Jason—Jason's voyage to procure his birthright, the throne, was a woolly one. This chief Argonaut and magnificent hero pursues the Golden Fleece in many thrilling episodes, as described by Apollonius of Rhodes in *The Argonautica* (third century B.C.) and in Virgil (first century A.D.), among other places. By contrast, neither of the Jasons in William Faulkner's *The Sound and the Fury* (1929) has qualities one would want repeated in one's offspring.

Menelaus—Helen's husband, the boisterous and aggressive ruler of Sparta and brother of Agamemnon, should have kept better track of his wife, according to *The Iliad* and *The Odyssey* by Homer (ninth century B.C.), and Euripides' fifth-century B.C. *Trojan Women,* among other places.

Odysseus—Odysseus is smart and brave, with a determination to get home that becomes epic in the hands of Homer in *The Iliad* and *The Odyssey* (ninth century B.C.). Odysseus is the author of great ideas such as the Trojan Horse. (*See* Ulysses.)

Oedipus Rex—A topic of fascination for the great fifth-century B.C. Greek tragedian Sophocles, the Theban Oedipus unwittingly sleeps with his mother, siring four children (Eteocles, Polynices, Antigone, and Ismeme). Later, equally in the dark, Oedipus slays his father. In penance, he blinds himself. He is also featured in Aeschylus' *The Seven Against Thebes* (467 B.C.). Oedipus' behavior is later pathologized by psychiatrists and becomes a "complex."

Orestes—Agamemnon and Clytemnestra's son avenges his father's murder by killing his mother and her lover, Aegisthus. A rough period follows as the Furies pursue him. Finally Athena rescues him in *The Oresteia* by Aeschylus (sixth century B.C.). Jean-Paul Sartre adopted the story of Orestes to his own existential purposes in *The Flies* (1943).

Orpheus—Calliope and Apollo's son, a poet and musician, bonds to Eurydice, a dryad, who dies of

 *O*VID

Ovid, poet and writer of first-century Rome, delivered literary history a tremendous gift by compiling a complete and marvelously entertaining mythology from the beginning of time forward. In fifteen volumes, this licentious man of letters immortalized the immortals—the gods, goddesses, heroes, and heroines other authors have since celebrated.

snakebite. To get her back, Orpheus plucks at his lyre before Hades, that head of the Underworld. Hades puts conditions on the parole, which Orpheus breaks. Eurydice is thus stuck in the land of the dead. Subsequently, Orpheus is too bereft to serve the Maenads, who then tear him asunder. His head washes up at Lesbos and, talking back, becomes an oracle, as recounted by Ovid in *Metamorphoses* (first century A.D.), Claudio Monteverdi's *Orfeo*

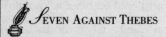 ## SEVEN AGAINST THEBES

Seven mythical champions depart Argos to help Polynices war against his brother Eteocles (both Oedipus' sons) for the throne of Thebes. In the story, Thebes has seven gates, one champion per. Find them in Aeschylus' The Seven Against Thebes (467 B.C.), Euripides' Phoenician Women (410 B.C.) and The Suppliants (490 B.C.), Seneca's Phoenissae, and Statius' Thebais (91 A.D.).

Adrastus
Amphiaraus
Tydeus
Pathenopaeus
Hippomedon
Capaneus
Polynices
Some versions substitute for Tydeus and Polynices:
Mecisteus
Eteoclus

(1607), Franz Joseph Haydn's *Orfeo* (1805), Christoph Gluck's *Orpheus and Eurydice* (1762), and Jean Cocteau's film *Orfée* (1950).

Paris—Paris, like most babies who were left to die but survive, proves resilient throughout life. Handsome, brash, stubborn, and smitten, he's the man who precipitates the downfall of Troy as recounted first in Homer's *The Iliad* and *The Odyssey* (ninth century B.C.). Aphrodite helps Paris abduct Helen of Troy after he awards the goddess the golden "apple of discord." In William Shakespeare's *Romeo and Juliet* (1596), Paris, whom Juliet dislikes, is the husband her father chooses for her.

Philoctetes—Philoctetes, a Greek soldier, incurs a snakebite that causes his fellow soldiers to abandon him. He ultimately kills Paris with one of Hercules' arrows, according to Homer's *The Iliad* and *The Odyssey* (ninth century B.C.).

Prometheus—Prometheus is the brave and well-intentioned Titan who fashions humans out of clay and sparks them to life with fire. As a result of this gift for combustion, Zeus chains him to a rock, where an eagle plucks at his liver . . . forever. The Athenian poet Aeschylus wrote the story in *Prometheus Bound* (sixth century B.C.). Percy Bysshe Shelley fixed this in *Prometheus Unbound* in 1820, wherein Prometheus finds a way to cease the liver picking and initiates an era of love.

Proteus—In Greek myths, Proteus changed shape at will. In Euripides' *Helen* (412 B.C.), he was the erstwhile king of Egypt. In William Shakespeare's *The Two Gentlemen of Verona* (1592), another Proteus is Valentine's rival for the hand of Silvia, in a caddish way.

Theseus—Theseus is heir to the throne of Athens whose numerable feats fed many legends and ancient tragedies. Sophocles has him defending Oedipus in *Oedipus at Colonus* (fifth century B.C.). In Geoffrey Chaucer's "The Knight's Tale" and William Shakespeare's *A Midsummer Night's Dream* (1595), he is the voice of reason. More recently, Mary Renault's *The King Must Die* (1958) and *The Bull from the Sea* (1962) retell his story.

Thyrsis—Thyrsis is the quintessential shepherd, appearing in Theocritus' *Idyls* (third century B.C.), Virgil's *Bucolics* (first century A.D.), and John Milton's "Allegro" (1638).

Tiresias—An influential Theban with second sight, which was good since he was blind, came upon two snakes coupling. He was for a while turned into a woman. Afterward, Tiresias was asked who more profoundly felt rapture, men or women, and he said women, by a margin of nine to one. Tiresias appears in Sophocles' *Oedipus* and *Antigone* and Aeschylus' *The Seven Against Thebes* (both fifth century B.C.) as well as in Apollinaire's *Les Mamelles de Tirèsias* (1917) and T. S. Eliot's *The Waste Land* (1922).

Tithonus—In *The Iliad* and *The Odyssey* (ninth century B.C.), Homer described Tithonus, a devastatingly handsome Trojan whose good looks bring him the gift of immortality. Though he never dies, he becomes so old and decrepit that the gods take pity on him and turn him into a songful, leg-rubbing grasshopper. Alfred, Lord Tennyson's nineteenth-century poem "Tithonus" repeats this story.

Troilus—Warrior son of Priam, king of Troy, makes a vow of eternal love to Criseyde. The story of Troilus' ill-fated adoration figured in the work of Virgil, Homer, Geoffrey Chaucer, and in William Shakespeare's *Troilus and Cressida* (1602).

Ulysses—Ulysses is the Latin name of the tireless homeward-bound hero of the Homeric epic *The Iliad* and *The Odyssey* (ninth century B.C.). It is also the subject and title of both a poem by Alfred, Lord Tennyson (1842) ("to strive, to seek, to find, and not to yield") and the 1922 novel by James Joyce.

FROM CRUSADES TO CASTLES:
Medieval Names (from the Dark Ages through the mid-sixteenth century)

❧ ⟋ ☙

𝓗AD non-Christian barbarians not descended from the north, literature might have stayed peopled with characters whose names were strictly French and Italian. But the tufty-locked, bloodthirsty Saxons, Angles, and Jutes invaded. They brought stories of warriors, gods, kings, and monsters and names that are stouter by their very pronunciation, as you'll read. In response to their wild ways, feudalism spread with Christianity, and literature, largely oral, in tow. A few great legend spinners submitted these tales to paper. They left a tantalizing legacy that writers throughout time have mined for ideas and characters.

Medieval Women's Names

Alcina—This alluring embodiment of eroticism turns her many lovers into flora and fauna in *Orlando*

Furioso (Mad Roland) by Lodovico Ariosto (1516), as should always happen after great sex.

Angelica—The captivating heroine Angelica, a pagan princess in *Orlando Innamorato (Roland in Love)* by Matteo Maria Boiardo (1487) and *Orlando Furioso (Mad Roland)* by Lodovico Ariosto (1516), has wiles to lead Charlemagne's paladins astray. The busy Angelica betrays Orlando then runs off with a Moor. Those Moors.

Badroulboudour—A pretty sultan's daughter in diaphanous garb, Badroulboudour marries Aladdin in *The Arabian Nights* (Persian folktales, circa 1450).

Beatrice—Beatrice is the object of Dante Alighieri's lifelong attachment and inspiration whose praises are sung in the *Vita Nuova (The New Life)* in 1290 and who is featured throughout his *Divine Comedy* (1314). She is later Leonato's wonderfully feisty niece in William Shakespeare's *Much Ado About Nothing* (1598). A scheming Beatrice suffers in love in Thomas Middleton and William Rowley's *The Changeling* (1623). Beatrice Cenci, featured in Percy Bysshe Shelley's *The Cenci* (1819), together with her mother and brothers, plots the death of her father. Her head rolls. Nathaniel Hawthorne wrote "Rappaccini's Daughter" (1844) about a botanical Beatrice raised on poisons to fortify her against calamitous toxins; however, Beatrice's lover gives her an "antidote" that kills her.

Blanchefleur—Blanchefleur is a medieval princess, torn from her lover, Floire, by Saracens and later saved in *Floire and Blanchefleur* (author and date unknown).

Bradamante—A warrior maiden, clad in white armor with a magical spear, is the object of Ruggiero's affection and ultimately his wife in *Orlando Innamorato (Roland in Love)* by Matteo Maria Boiardo (1487) and *Orlando Furioso (Mad Roland)* by Lodovico Ariosto (1516).

TEN PEOPLE, TEN DAYS, AND INFINITE ENJOYMENT

Giovanni Boccaccio (1313–75), reputedly the illegitimate son of a French noblewoman and Florentine merchant, wrote the finest work of pure fiction in the Italian Renaissance, The Decameron. *These one hundred stories were supposedly exchanged between ten people who sequestered themselves against the plague at a villa in the country, over a period of ten days. Boccaccio borrowed from classical sources, French fables, and folklore to create colorful characters and plotlines that vary between tragedy and comedy. The then king of Naples's illegitimate daughter, Maria de Conti d'Aquino, was Boccaccio's mistress, and their relationship fueled his imagination during years in Naples. Later, in Florence and Venice, he relied on his strong friendship with Petrarch, both for literary and emotional support. His stories and characters became a source of inspiration for authors of coming centuries.*

Canacee—In Geoffrey Chaucer's "The Squire's Tale," among *The Canterbury Tales* (1390), Canacee has a ring that allows her to speak to birds. Canacee is a fair and modest lady whom many knights fight over in Edmund Spenser's *The Faerie Queen* (1590–96).

Cecilia—In Geoffrey Chaucer's "The Second Nun's Tale," among *The Canterbury Tales* (1390), Cecilia is guarded by an angel who gives her a crown of roses. A blind Roman woman who is a wonderful musician, Cecilia is visited by an angel and beatified. John Dryden and Alexander Pope both wrote odes to her around this time. Cecilia Beverly is one of Fanny Burney's young creations. In *Cecilia* (1782), she hopes to shore up her family's diminishing prestige by marriage to a man who will take her name, not an easy trick.

Clothilde—Clovis's queen, originator of the fleur-de-lis, is featured in medieval literature.

Dorigen—Geoffrey Chaucer wrote of Dorigen, Arveragus' faithful wife in *The Canterbury Tales* (1390). Her fidelity wins a bargain for him.

Deidre—Like most extraordinary beauties, Deidre is a magnet for death and destruction, including her own. She bashes her head against a rock in an *Ulster Cycle* folktale of the Middle Ages.

Emily—Emily is the unspeakably beautiful object of nearly everyone's infatuation in Boccaccio's *Tes-*

eida (1351), reappearing with the same magnetism in one of Geoffrey Chaucer's *The Canterbury Tales* (1390). Emilie was the given name of Madame Gabrielle du Châtelet, a French physicist to whom Voltaire wrote poetry (1723 to 1749). Emily Grierson, William Faulkner's character in "A Rose for Emily," keeps the corpse of her suitor Homer Barron in a closet for many years, misusing valuable storage space. Emily Webb, insightful and frank, returns from the dead to reexamine her life in Thornton Wilder's play *Our Town* (1938). Kurt Vonnegut evokes a dead but previously dazzling Emily Hoenikker in *Cat's Cradle* (1963).

Enide—In an Arthurian romance by Chrétien de Troyes, Erec abandons his knight-life to marry Enide. She soon becomes bored with their humdrum existence, so he whisks her off to many adventures in *Erec and Enide* (twelfth century). In "Geraint and Enid" from Alfred, Lord Tennyson's *Idylls of the King* (1859–85), Enid represents the "true woman," obedient to the demands of her husband, perhaps not so popular a notion these days. Tennyson wrote that her beauty varied like the heaven's light and that what she did, she did to please her husband's eye.

Elaine—Elaine is the pretty but conniving young woman who tricks Lancelot into sleeping with her, a coupling that yields Galahad in Sir Thomas Malory's *Le Morte d'Arthur* (1469). In "Lancelot and Elaine" from Alfred, Lord Tennyson's *Idylls of the*

King (1859–85), and again in his "The Lady of Shalott," Elaine dies of love.

Fiammetta—Impassioned over Maria d'Aquino, Giovanni Boccaccio called her "Fiammetta" and made her his muse. With her name eliciting darting flames of passion, she presides over his fourteenth-century stories. *L'Amorosa Fiammetta* (1340–45) describes his obsession.

Francesca—One of Dante's adulterous lovers in the *Inferno* (1315), she deceives again in Stephen Phillips's *Paolo and Francesca* (1900) and again in *Francesca da Rimini* (1901) by Gabriele d'Annunzio. In these stories, Francescas seem drawn to men named Paolo.

Ginevra—Bernabo's quick-thinking wife has a gift for survival in Giovanni Boccaccio's *The Decameron* (1351). William Shakespeare borrowed her for *Cymbeline* (1609).

Gráinne—Gráinne is the second wife of Fionn mac Cumhail (Finn MacCool), legendary Irish character of the *Fenian Cycle* folktales. Gráinne runs off with Diarmud, whom Finn pursues into the wilderness, of which there was plenty in the third century B.C. She appears much later in James Macpherson's (Ossian) epic poem *Fingal* (1762).

Griselda—Griselda is a wife of unparalleled constancy, masochism, and patience in Giovanni Boccaccio's *The Decameron* (1351). Geoffrey Chaucer borrowed her story for *The Canterbury Tales* (1390).

Guenever (Guinevere, Guenevere)—This lady, King Arthur's lovely, warm, and cuckolding wife, was immortalized by several writers, most notably Sir Thomas Malory in *Le Morte d'Arthur* (1469); also in William Morris's poem "The Defence of Guenevere" (1858).

Isabel (Isabella)—Originally in Giovanni Boccaccio's *The Decameron* (1351), Isabella disinters her lover Lorenzo's severed head and buries it in her basil pot, which she irrigates with tears. She reappears in John Keats's *Isabella* (1820), gardening with the same ingenuity. Isabella is also William Shakespeare's comely and powerfully devout novice in *Measure for Measure* (1604). She is as well the damsel in distress in Horace Walpole's *The Castle of Otranto* (1764). Lady Isabel Vane in Mrs. Henry Wood's *East Lynne* (1861) follows her passions only to lose her children, a common pitfall. Henry James's independent but idealistic Isabel Archer is in *The Portrait of a Lady* (1881).

Iseult (Isolde)—Iseult is a lovely charmer, in every sense of the word, with a gift for healing. She and Tristram inadvertently quaff a love potion leaving them forever intoxicated with one another. Of Celtic origin, they are found in the medieval cycle *Tristan and Iseult,* Sir Thomas Malory's *Le Morte d'Arthur* (1469), Tennyson's *Idylls of the King* (1859–85), Edwin Arlington Robinson's *Tristram* (1927), and numerous other places.

Jeanne (Joan)—Thanks to fifteenth-century Joan of Arc, the names Jeanne and Joan call to mind the consummate female martyr, consumed by passion for her cause and her God. Jeanne/Joan reappears again and again throughout literature. Friedrich von Schiller portrays her determined vision in *Joan of Arc* (1801). Heroine Jeanie Deans in Sir Walter Scott's *The Heart of Midlothian* (1818) walks from Edinburgh to London to save her sister Effie.

Kriemhild—Kriemhild is the fabulous Siegfried's love interest in *The Nibelungenlied* (written by an anonymous Austrian poet c. 1200) who benefits from his magic cape.

Laura—In the 1300s, Laura is the unattainable and exquisite object of Francesco Petrarch's neurotic moral conflict—to make love or just to think about it? Admiration for Petrarch and the lyricism of the word "Laura" itself carried her name forward into literature for centuries to come—in Robert Tofte's *Laura* (1597), Frederick von Schiller's *Laura* poems of the 1790s, and Lord Byron's *Beppo* (1818). Tennessee Williams's troubled Laura retires into a world of glass whatnots in *The Glass Menagerie* (1944).

Lynette—(Liones) Lynette is a damsel rescued by Sir Gareth in Sir Thomas Malory's *Le Morte d'Arthur* (1469) and in "Gareth and Lynette," from Alfred, Lord Tennyson's *Idylls of the King* (1859–85).

Marion (Marian)—Over time, chroniclers of Robin Hood have always made mention of his main squeeze, the resourceful and loyal Maid Marion. Victor Hugo's *Marion de Lorme* (1829) is the story of a seventeenth-century courtesan. Willa Cather created Marian Forrester, a delightful woman tossed about by life's fortunes and misfortunes in *A Lost Lady* (1923).

May—In Geoffrey Chaucer's *The Canterbury Tales* (1390), May plays a perfidious young wife in "The Merchant's Tale." Sweet, proper, and predictable May Welland is betrothed to Newland Archer in Edith Wharton's *The Age of Innocence* (1920) and their future together appears a total yawn.

Melissa—Melissa is a prophetess and magician who lives in Merlin's grotto in Lodovico Ariosto's *Orlando Furioso (Mad Roland)* (1516).

Melusina—Melusina is a mermaid who can remain human for her human lover, except on Sundays when she worships with a tail, in *Melusina* (1387) by Jean d'Arras.

Morgan (Morgaine, Morgana)—King Arthur's exquisite but wicked half sister Morgan le Fay is sometimes associated with the Lady of the Lake. She tricks Arthur into the sack, which results in their double recessive dud son, Mordred . . . who brings down Camelot. Despite Morgan's damage to Arthur, it is she who transports him to Avalon for healing after the final battle in Sir Thomas Malory's in *Le Morte d'Arthur* (1469). Marion Zimmer Bradley wrote *The Mists of Avalon* (1987) about King Arthur's half sister. Her Morgaine hung out with the faeries and was a mystical person, capable of the "sight."

Nicolette—Nicolette is a Saracen slave whose deep love for Aucassin, the count of Beaucaire, is the basis of the thirteenth-century fable *Aucassin and Nicolette* (author unknown).

Nimuë—Nimuë is the mysterious Lady of the Lake who lured Merlin to his watery death. (She is also known as Vivien in some versions.) Both Lancelot and Excalibur issued from her depths according to Sir Thomas Malory's *Le Morte d'Arthur* (1469) and Alfred, Lord Tennyson's *Idylls of the King* (1859–85).

---

*S*CANDINAVIAN GODS AND GODDESSES

These gods appear in poems between 700 and 1070 A.D. The oral legends about them were not written down until late in this era, by Icelander Snorri Sturluson (1179–1241) in the Edda, of 1222. Snorri Sturluson was the son of a powerful chieftain, and though his life was largely devoted to culture, his heated involvement in politics embroiled him in violent power struggles, not only in Iceland but also in Norway. His depictions of Scandinavian mythology are therefore a personal expression of the Norse soul. Ultimately, the Norwegian king had Snorri killed. The names seem austere, with mysterious undertones, like the Scandinavian climate.

Odin—This god of all gods, and of warriors, is arrogant and stern, the quintessential patriarchal figure.

Frigg (Frigga)—Odin's wife, goddess of all gods, is independent, intelligent, and queenly. As a fertility goddess,

she is also concerned with women and children. Frigg is
also beautiful and psychic.

Bragi—The god of poetry, Bragi welcomes all fallen heroes
to Valhalla. He is Odin and Frigg's son.

Thunor—Thunor is god of the thunderstorm, also known
as Thor. Though a bit thick, Thunor is good-natured,
huge, and immensely strong. Having a tendency to tem-
peramental outbursts, he usually carries a hammer.

Heimdall—Heimdall is the Scandinavian god who watches
over heaven, listening to grass grow. Like some children,
when he blasts his magical horn, it is heard throughout
the universe (eighth century).

Sif—Goddess of the crop and harvest, wife of Thunor, Sif
becomes dark and sullen when her long golden locks are
hacked off and stolen. Who wouldn't? Her pouting con-
tinues through the winter while they grow back.

Tiu—Tiu is the god of the sky and of war.

Balder—The Norse god of the sun, Balder is all innocence
and light, later described by William Morris's *Funeral
of Balder*, Robert Buchanan's *Balder the Beautiful*, and
Henry Wadsworth Longfellow's "Tegner's Drapa."

Freja—Freja is the Norse goddess of erotic love and marriage, a woman fond of luxury.

Njord—Njord is the god of the sea who cannot live without
the smell and sounds of the deep. Importantly to the
Norsemen, he is the protector of mariners.

Sabrina—Sabrina is the charming daughter of Estrildi and Locrine in Geoffrey of Monmouth's *History of the King of Britain* (1137). In John Milton's *Comus* (1634), Sabina is a river nymph.

Scheherazade—Wife of the sultan of India spins riveting stories of *The Arabian Nights* (Persion folktales, circa 1450) to prevent the sultan from having her put to death.

Sedb—Sedb is the first wife of Fionn mac Cumhail (Finn MacCool), the legendary Irish hero of the *Fenian Cycle* (third century B.C.). She appears much later in James Macpherson's epic poem *Fingal* (1762).

Vivien—Vivien is the mysterious Lady of the Lake who lured Merlin to his watery death. Both Lancelot and Excalibur issued from her depths according to Sir Thomas Malory's *Le Morte d'Arthur* (1469) and Alfred, Lord Tennyson's *Idylls of the King* (1859–85). (She is known as Nimuë in some versions.)

Wealhtheow—In *Beowulf* (author unknown, eighth century), Grendel menaces Hrothgar's wise and gracious wife, the queen of the Scyldings. Wealhtheow means "peaceweaver."

Medieval Men's Names

Ahmed—Ahmed is a prince, happily armed with tricks up his sleeve, such as the magic carpet in *The Arabian Nights* (Persian folktales, circa 1450).

Aladdin—Aladdin is a tireless urchin who goes from rags to riches in *The Arabian Nights* (Persian folktales, circa 1450).

Ali Baba—The resourceful woodcutter becomes fabulously wealthy by way of the forty thieves and saying "open sesame" in *The Arabian Nights* (Persian folktales, circa 1450).

Arthur—Wise, just king of all England, Arthur is desirous of peace, though not without bravery. He is the hero of Sir Thomas Malory's *Le Morte d'Arthur* (1469) and Alfred, Lord Tennyson's poem of the same name (1842). In William Shakespeare's *King John* (1596), Arthur, obligated by heritage to pursue the throne of England, prefers the simple life. Arthur Dimmesdale is the well-spoken and respectful minister of Nathaniel Hawthorne's *The Scarlet Letter* (1850), who also happens to be the man responsible for Hester's *A*. Another Arthur with unlaced pants is the no-account squire Arthur Donnithorne in George Eliot's *Adam Bede* (1859). In 1905, H. G. Wells wrote *Kipps,* a novel about Arthur Kipps, whose life runs entirely afoul when he inherits a mother lode. Not until he is again humble does the book find a happy ending.

Arveragus—Arveragus is a slave to his wife, so in love is he, in Geoffrey Chaucer's *The Canterbury Tales* (1390).

Astolfo—Astolfo is one of Charlemagne's most handsome, courteous, and boastful minions. As a Carolingian paladin, Astolfo goes all the way to the moon in search of Roland's lost wits. He is featured in *Orlando Innamorato (Roland in Love)* by Matteo Maria Boiardo (1487) and *Orlando Furioso (Mad Roland)* by Lodovico Ariosto (1516).

Aucassin—Aucassin is a count who will not be separated from his true love, Nicolette. Their obsession is the basis of the thirteenth-century fable *Aucassin and Nicolette* (author unknown).

Beowulf—The bold Scandinavian prince is hero of the eighth-century story by the same name, author not known. In three episodes, strong, brave Beowulf tears out the monster Grendel's arm then slays Grendel's mother, and finishes fifty years later by leveling a fire-breathing dragon, but not before the dragon mortally wounds him.

Bernabò—Ginevra's overly confident husband brags of his wife, which ultimately leads to several bad years, in "Bernabò of Genoa" from Giovanni Boccaccio's *The Decameron* (1351). All ends well, however.

Bors—Bors is a noble knight of the Round Table, Lancelot's uncle, and one granted sight of the Holy Grail in Sir Thomas Malory's *Le Morte d'Arthur* (1469).

Brute—One of Aeneas' great-grandsons, Brute lands in England and calls Britain after his own name in Geoffrey of Monmouth's *History of the Kings of Britain* (1137).

Canute—Danish king and then king of England, remarkable for his modesty and his ability to maintain

peace, Canute is remembered in the twelfth-century
lyric *The Song of Canute*.

Dante—Author and protagonist in Dante Alighieri's
political and theological allegorical poem, *The Divine Comedy*, he is eloquent and gifted, a strong
political figure.

Damyan—In Geoffrey Chaucer's *The Canterbury
Tales* (1390), Damyan is a robust young squire.

Erec—In an Arthurian romance by Chrétien de
Troyes, Erec abandons his knight-life to marry Enide. She soon becomes bored with their humdrum
existence, so he whisks her off to many adventures
in *Erec and Enide* (twelfth century).

Fergus—Fergus is a stalwart Gaelic warrior featured
first in ancient Irish literature in the *Ulster Cycle*,
pagan romances of the Middle Ages.

Fierbras—One of Charlemagne's paladins, Fierbras is
an enormous man converted to Christianity on the
battlefield by Olivier in *Orlando Innamorato (Roland in Love)* by Matteo Maria Boiardo (1487) and
Orlando Furioso (Mad Roland) by Lodovico Ariosto (1516).

Fionn (Finn)—Fionn mac Cumhail, or Finn MacCool
as he is called, is the legendary Irish hero of the
Fenian Cycle (third century B.C.), an exceptionally
robust man who lives in the forest. He appears much
later in James Macpherson's epic poem *Fingal*
(1762).

Floire—This medieval prince is raised with a little princess, Blanchefleur. Later he pursues her captors throughout the Orient, compelled by love to save her in *Floire and Blanchefleur* (author and date unknown).

Franklin—In *The Canterbury Tales* by fourteenth-century English poet Geoffrey Chaucer, the Franklin is that rare breed of the Middle Ages, neither a vassal nor a noble. A "free man," the Franklin is a connoisseur of food and wine.

Galahad—The most virtuous knight of the Round Table, Lancelot's son Galahad finds the long-lost Holy Grail. As finding valuable lost objects is an indispensable skill, Galahad is a noble name. His accomplishments are featured in Sir Thomas Malory's *Le Morte d'Arthur* (1469), in "Sir Galahad" from Alfred, Lord Tennyson's *Idylls of the King* (1859–1885), and in Mark Twain's *A Connecticut Yankee in King Arthur's Court* (1889).

Gareth—As a lad, Gareth begs entry into King Arthur's circle, claiming his name is "Beaumains." This is by virtue of his sizable hands, a feature that still demands respect. As a knight, Gareth performs gloriously, freeing and marrying Lynette (also known as Liones). When Lancelot inadvertently kills him, it precipitates the downfall of the court. Described in Sir Thomas Malory's *Le Morte d'Arthur* (1469) and "Gareth and Lynette," from Alfred, Lord Tennyson's *Idylls of the King* (1859–1885).

Gawain—Loyal, courteous, and bursting with honor, he is the hero of *Sir Gawain and the Green Knight* (Arthurian legend of the late fourteenth century) and appears in Sir Thomas Malory's *Le Morte d'Arthur* (1469). Among his noble deeds, he somehow manages to resist the amorous entreaties of King Bercilak's wanton wife.

Grendel—Accursed monster, half man, half fiend, descendant of Cain, first object of Beowulf's attention, Grendel only works as a name selection when children are naughty.

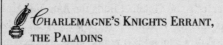 *C*HARLEMAGNE'S KNIGHTS ERRANT, THE PALADINS

From La Chanson de Roland *(author unknown, eleventh century),* Orlando Innamorato (Roland in Love) *by Matteo Maria Boiardo (1487), and* Orlando Furioso (Mad Roland) *by Lodovico Ariosto (1516)*

Anseis	Ivon
Astolfo	Ivory
Berengier	Namo
Engelier	Ogier
Fierabras	Olivier
Florismart	Otton
Ganalon	Rinaldo
Gerard	Roland
Gerier	Samson
Gerin	Turpin

Guy—Guy is a busy medieval knight who turns hermit in order to slow down in *Guy of Warwick* (c. 1300). Guy Mannering, in a Sir Walter Scott novel by the same name (1815), is fascinated with astrology. He predicts two crises in a boy's life that put the rest of the novel into motion. Ray Bradbury's Guy Montag follows his conscience, often rashly, and turns to books for illumination in *Fahrenheit 451* (1953).

Harry—Geoffrey Chaucer's innkeeper, Harry Bailly, serves as a judge in the storytelling contest, *The Canterbury Tales* (1390). Harry is the disappearing son in Sir Walter Scott's *Guy Mannering* (1815), who reappears as a Captain Brown. Harry "Rabbit" Angstrom is John Updike's American everyman in *Rabbit, Run* (1961), *Rabbit Redux* (1971), and *Rabbit Is Rich* (1981).

Hermann (also Arminius)—Hermann was sort of a Che Guevara of Roman Germany, celebrated in many works as a preserver of Teutonic heritage. He is the subject of several German dramas in the last half of the eighteenth and early nineteenth century.

Hrothgar—This "good king was he" leader of the Scyldings endures the ravaging of his kingdom by Grendel in *Beowulf*.

Launcelot (Lancelot)—Lancelot is the most chivalrous and undefeated knight of the Round Table. His one gaffe, becoming Guinevere's lover, turns out to be a considerable one. He is featured frequently, most prominently in Sir Thomas Malory's *Le Morte d'Arthur* (1469) and also in "Lancelot and Elaine," a poem from Alfred, Lord Tennyson's *Idylls of the King* (1859–85).

Launfal—Sir Launfal is an Arthurian knight who dares to love a beautiful faerie instead of Guenevere in *Breton Lai* by Marie de France (twelfth century).

Lohengrin—Lohengrin comes swooping into Antwerp on a swan-pulled skiff to make off with Elsa's heart and hand. Irritatingly, he can only marry her if she promises not to ask his name or identity. As she cannot contain herself, he is forced to leave her . . . and on their wedding night, too, in Wolfram von Eschenbach's *Parzival* (1210).

Lucifer—Though euphonious, Lucifer is a helluva moniker. Find him in Dante's *Inferno* (1315) and Christopher Marlowe's *The Tragical History of Doctor Faustus* (1589–1604), After a fall from heaven, Lucifer is renamed "Satan," one of the greatest literary characters of all time in *Paradise Lost* by John Milton (1667).

Merlin—A venerable seer, Merlin is Arthur's counselor in *Le Morte d'Arthur* (1469) by Sir Thomas Malory. He appears in many other works throughout literary history.

Mordred—A sly devil, Mordred is not a good name for someone you love. This bastard child of King Arthur and his half sister Morgan le Fay succeeds in toppling the Round Table and Arthur's reign in Sir Thomas Malory's *Le Morte d'Arthur* (1469) and elsewhere.

Naisi—Deidre's valiant savior and lover in an *Ulster Cycle* folktale of the Middle Ages, Naisi dies along with her.

Oísin—Oísin is the son of Sedb and Fionn mac Cumhail (Finn MacCool), legendary Irish character of the *Fenian Cycle* (third century B.C.). He appears much later in James Macpherson's epic poem *Fingal* (1762).

Olivier—Charlemagne's sworn friend and paladin, remarkable for his common sense, Olivier is featured in *Orlando Innamorato (Roland in Love)* by Matteo Maria Boiardo (1487) and *Orlando Furioso (Mad Roland)* by Lodovico Ariosto (1516).

Paolo—Paolos should be kept away from women named Francesca. Paolo is one of Dante's adulterous lovers in the *Inferno* (1315), who deceives again in Stephen Phillips's *Paolo and Francesca* (1900) and again in *Francesca da Rimini* (1901) by Gabriele d'Annunzio.

Paribanou—Paribanou is a fairy in *The Arabian Nights* (Persian folktales, circa 1450).

Parsifal (Parzifal, Percival, Perceval)—As a young man, this aspiring knight is sympathetic but clumsy. He eventually becomes an indispensable member of King Arthur's Round Table in the search for the Holy Grail in *Le Conte du Graal* by Chrétien de Troyes (1175), Sir Thomas Malory's *Le Morte d'Arthur* (1469), *Parzifal* (c. 1210) by Wolfram von Eschenbach, and Alfred, Lord Tennyson's *Idylls of the King* (1859–85). Also, as a character referred to in Virginia Woolf's *The Waves* (1931), Percival epitomizes the balanced and good-natured spirit.

Piers—Piers is the plowman hero of the allegorical dream vision *Piers Plowman,* written in the fourteenth century, probably by William Langland. The charitable Piers cultivates his land for the activity itself rather than for profit, in contrast to the corrupt clergy of the time. Not the aggressive type, Piers has been compared to Jesus.

Robin—Robin Hood made it his habit to rob from the rich to give to the poor. The legend is first mentioned in *Piers Plowman* (1377) and many times since. Robin Goodfellow, the mischievous nocturnal Puck, is a feral sprite in *A Midsummer Night's Dream* (1594) by William Shakespeare.

Roderick—Roderick or Rodrigo is a brave and pious Visigoth king according to a legend dating from the eighth century. His is also the first name of the virtuous and heroic El Cid. Roderick's adventures appear in the twelfth-century *Historia Roderici* and shortly after in *The Song of the Cid.* Pierre Corneille wrote the tragedy *Le Cid* in 1637. A Roderigo plays the lackey for Iago in William Shakespeare's *Othello* (1604). In Tobias George Smollett's comedic novel *The Adventures of Roderick Random* (1748), Roderick is a disinherited rascal who ricochets from one scrape to another but lands well and "landed." Edgar Allan Poe described a hypersensitive character, "if ever mortal painted an ideal that mortal was Roderick Usher," whose visions of his dead sister presage his own downfall in "The Fall of the

House of Usher" (1839). *Roderick Hudson* (1876) is an American sculptor with a painful attraction to Christina Light, created by Henry James.

Rodomonte—This Saracen hero is called the "Mars of Africa." He fights against invading Christians in *Orlando Innamorato (Roland in Love)* by Matteo Maria Boiardo (1487) and *Orlando Furioso (Mad Roland)* by Lodovico Ariosto (1516).

Roland—*La Chanson de Roland* is an eleventh-century romance depicting Charlemagne's nephew's campaigns. Valiant and dauntless, Roland has a fancy sword and horn. Known in Italy as Orlando, he inspired *Orlando Innamorato (Roland in Love)* by Matteo Maria Boiardo (1487) and *Orlando Furioso (Mad Roland)* by Lodovico Ariosto (1516).

Ruggiero—Ruggiero is a pagan, suckled by lions in infancy. A warrior, he is eventually converted to Christianity in *Orlando Innamorato (Roland in Love)* by Matteo Maria Boiardo (1487) and *Orlando Furioso (Mad Roland)* by Lodovico Ariosto (1516).

Schahriah—Scheherazade's sultan, whose poor view of women inspires her to preserve her life in *The Arabian Nights* by telling stories (Persian folktales, circa 1450). After a thousand and one installments, he at last recognizes that she is supreme among her sex.

Siegfried—Gifted and brave Siegfried, hero of *The Nibelungenlied* (written by an anonymous Austrian poet c. 1200), can become invisible when wrapped in his magic cape. He is almost invincible, having been drenched in magical dragon blood in all but one spot.

Sinbad—Famously enterprising, Sinbad is the ocean-going merchant from *The Arabian Nights* (Persian folktales, circa 1450).

Titus—We have two entirely different Tituses. The first is a decent chap in "Titus and Gisippus" in Giovanni Boccaccio's *The Decameron* (1351). He at first profits from the selflessness of his friend Gisippus and in the end saves him. The second is William Shakespeare's gore-torn hero in *Titus Andronicus* (1590). His horrendous life drives him to inventive forms of revenge, including humans baked in a pie.

Tristram (Tristan)—Tristram is a superlative male specimen, a knight who, together with Iseult, inadvertently quaffs a love potion that leaves them forever in love. Of Celtic origin, they are found in the medieval cycle *Tristan and Iseult,* Sir Thomas Malory's *Le Morte d'Arthur* (1469), Alfred, Lord Tennyson's *Idylls of the King* (1859–85), Edwin Arlington Robinson's *Tristram* (1927), and numerous other works.

Tuck—First mentioned in *Piers Plowman* (1377) and many times hence, Friar Tuck is Robin Hood's broad-girthed, stout-hearted Franciscan monk friend. He also makes an appearance in Sir Walter Scott's *Ivanhoe* (1819).

Valerian—In Geoffrey Chaucer's "The Second Nun's Tale," one of *The Canterbury Tales* (1390), Cecilia's groom, Valerian, is guarded by an angel who gives him a crown of lilies.

Wiglaf—Beowulf's dauntless companion, loyal to the end in *Beowulf*.

THE ELIZABETHAN INSPIRATION:

Elizabethan Names (from the mid-sixteenth century through the 1620s)

⮞⮞ ⮜⮜

*T*HESE names show Europe shaking off its feudal slumber. They shimmer as the Continent did then, suddenly vibrating with ardent intellectual life. You'll find that the Elizabethan period, characterized by the long reign of the Virgin Queen herself, added poetry and sensuality to the Renaissance. In contrast, the Reformation fomented religious controversy and moralizing. Writers of this period borrowed heavily from mythology and channeled their energy into passionate and lively verse for expression and entertainment, of which Shakespeare is of course the greatest example.

Elizabethan Women's Names

Ariel—Ariel is a fairy, symbolizing high-flown idealism in William Shakespeare's *The Tempest* (1611). Sylvia Plath's collected poems by this title (1965) are considered invocations to death.

Armida—Armida is a captivating sorceress with a magical girdle that is more than merely ornamental, in *Jerusalem Liberated* by Torquato Tasso (1581).

Bianca—Bianca is Katharina's good-natured but Milquetoast sister in William Shakespeare's *The Taming of the Shrew* (1593).

Britomart—In Edmund Spenser's *The Faerie Queen* (1590–96), Britomart is the equivalent of Lady Chastity, in contrast to Malecasta (lust).

Calpurnia—Calpurnia is Julius Caesar's insightful wife who has a prophetic dream in William Shakespeare's *Julius Caesar* (1599).

Campaspe—Campaspe's many charms tug at Alexander's heartstrings in John Lyly's *Alexander and Campaspe* (1581).

Celia—Celia is Rosalind's great friend in William Shakespeare's *As You Like It* (1598). Find another Celia, Corvino's winsome and innocent wife, in Ben Jonson's *Volpone* (1606).

Cleopatra—The exceptionally beautiful, imperious, scheming, and greedy queen of Egypt nonetheless sincerely loves Marc Antony as she appears in William Shakespeare's *Antony and Cleopatra* (1606) and in John Dryden's *All for Love* (1678). Keep children of this name away from asps.

Clorinda—Clorinda is the fair-skinned daughter of an Ethiopian king. She is raised by a eunuch and suckled by a tiger, following which she falls in love with a crusader named Tancred who inadvertently kills her, as so often happens when one messes with weapons in the dark. Before she dies, she converts to Christianity and has time to rescue Olindo and his lover Sofronia from the stake, in *Jerusalem Delivered* by Torquato Tasso (1581).

Cordelia—Cordelia is the soft-spoken and sweet daughter of William Shakespeare's *King Lear* (1605), so sincere that she cannot flatter, for which inability she is disinherited. Though short-shrifted, she is not ruthless as are her two sisters, Goneril and Regan. Mystery writer P. D. James created an admirable young female sleuth named Cordelia Gray (1972–86).

Corinna—Ovid celebrated a Corinna in his first-century poetry, and people speculate that she was a favorite among his many lovers. "Corinna" is the lyric-voiced singer of a sixteenth-century poem by Thomas Campion, also the fresh, sweet object of a seventeenth-century poem by Robert Herrick, "Corinna's Going A-Maying."

Delia—Samuel Daniel wrote a sonnet sequence entitled *Delia* (1592) about a woman of boundless virtues.

Desdemona—In William Shakespeare's *Othello* (1604), Othello's good, pure, and devoted wife, Desdemona, is done in.

Dulcinea—Don Quixote's glorified name for the peasant trollop Aldonza in Miguel de Cervantes's

Don Quixote de la Mancha (1605). Quixote sees in her an amalgam of all glorious ideals.

Eleanor (Elinor)—King John's mother in William Shakespeare's drama *King John* (1596), she fiercely champions her son's cause. A model of restraint, Elinor Dashwood represents good sense in Jane Austen's *Sense and Sensibility* (1811).

Emilia—Emilia is Iago's incisive wife and Desdemona's faithful servant and companion in William Shakespeare's *Othello* (1604). Another Emilia is Theseus' sister-in-law, love object of two knights, Palamon and Arcite, in Giovanni Boccaccio's *Teseida* (around 1340) and later in John Fletcher's *The Two Noble Kinsmen* (1634). Percy Bysshe Shelley wrote *Epipsychidion* (1821) to a real Emilia, Emilia Viviani, who was in a convent against her will though "Epipsychidion," which means "this soul out of my soul," seems too big a mouthful for a name. Emilia is the subject of a poem by George Meredith, *Emilia in England* (1864).

Erminia—Erminia is a Syrian maiden who falls for Tancred when he spares her life. She develops a knack for nursing the wounded in *Jerusalem Delivered* by Torquato Tasso (1581).

Flavia—Flavia is a cunning and beguiling character in John Lyly's *Euphues*. The hero of Anthony Hope's *The Prisoner of Zenda* (1894) surrenders the hand of the lovely and beloved Princess Flavia.

Gertrude—Gertrude is Hamlet's mother, a weak and dependent woman in William Shakespeare's *Hamlet* (1602).

Gloriana—Gloriana is Edmund Spenser's name for Queen Elizabeth in *The Faerie Queen* (1590–96).

Helena—Helena is a bit trampy, a bit catty in William Shakespeare's *A Midsummer Night's Dream* (1594). On the other hand, she is a persistent and resourceful young woman with many lovable qualities in *All's Well That Ends Well* (1610).

"*My* Project Was to Please"

William Shakespeare (1564–1616), the greatest dramatist ever born, left what is perhaps the West's greatest literary bounty in his Sonnets and thirty-eight plays, some of which were collaborations. Though they were performed before the courts of Elizabeth I and James I, and Shakespeare shared in the profits of the Globe and the Blackfriars theaters, his work was thought by some contemporaries to be somewhat vulgar. Much influenced by Seneca, Thomas Kyd, and Christopher Marlowe, they were at once political, insouciant, sordid, and glorious.

That he used poetry to express the full range of humanity is his greatest achievement. He often reused names, attaching them to a benevolent character in one play and a malevolent character in another. This duality emphasizes the broad characteristics any good name can encompass.

Hermia—Hermia is resistant to authority in the face
of love in William Shakespeare's *A Midsummer
Night's Dream* (1594).

Hero—This priestess of Aphrodite's devotion to her
lover, Leander, led her to throw herself into the sea
after he drowned trying to swim the Hellespont to
get to her. This myth was made popular in a work
by Christopher Marlowe, completed by George
Chapman after Marlowe's death. Hero is also Beatrice's sweet relative who falls immediately for
Claudio in William Shakespeare's *Much Ado About
Nothing* (1598).

Imogen—This smart, resourceful, and beautiful British princess marries Posthumus despite her father's
objection in William Shakespeare's *Cymbeline*
(1609). She looks great in trousers.

Irena—Irena, who represents Ireland, approaches the
court of *The Faerie Queen* (1590–96) to protest
Grantorto (great wrong), as described by Edmund
Spenser.

Julia—Julia is Proteus's doting love who dresses up
as his page in William Shakespeare's *The Two Gentlemen of Verona* (1592). In George Orwell's *1984*
(1944), Winston's upbeat lover, Julia, strategizes
her sexual exploits in the midst of Big Brother's
surveillance.

Juliet—Possibly literature's most passionate lover, Juliet is also a disobedient daughter in William Shakespeare's *Romeo and Juliet* (1596). A less known

Juliet, Claudio's lover, a bit premature in her favors, is found in William Shakespeare's *Measure for Measure* (1604).

Katharina (Katerina, Kate)—Though comely, Katharina or "Kate" is a fiery willful harridan, eventually subdued by Petruchio in William Shakespeare's *The Taming of the Shrew* (1593). Katerina Ivanovna is Dmitri's sanctimonious wife in Fyodor Dostoyevsky's *Brothers Karamazov* (1879–80). Henry James's Kate Croy is a manipulative lover whose plans founder in *The Wings of the Dove* (1902).

Luciana—Luciana is desired by the wandering Antipholus of Syracuse in William Shakespeare's *The Comedy of Errors* (1594) in which all ends happily.

Mab—Mab is the tantalizing and mischievous queen of the faeries, "midwife" in the delivery of dreams in William Shakespeare's *Romeo and Juliet* (1596) and in the "Allegro" (1632) of John Milton. Percy Bysshe Shelley wrote "Queen Mab" (1813) about the queen in her time chariot.

Margaret—Hero's maidservant in William Shakespeare's *Much Ado About Nothing* (1598) is named Margaret. Erasmus's flame-haired mother, Margaret, is thwarted in her love for his father, Gerard, in *The Cloister and the Hearth* (1861) by Charles Reade.

Maria—Maria is an irrepressible little trouble causer in William Shakespeare's *Twelfth Night* (1606). In Ernest Hemingway's *For Whom the Bell Tolls*

(1940), American Robert Jordan falls in love with a Spanish rape victim named Maria.

Marina—Pericles and Thaisa's daughter, born at sea, she is raised as an aristocrat and has to defend her honor vigorously when sold into prostitution in William Shakespeare's *Pericles, Prince of Tyre* (1604).

Miranda—Miranda is Prospero's innocent and unsullied daughter in William Shakespeare's *The Tempest* (1611). Miranda is a young woman of growing awareness whose observations lead her to journalism in Katherine Anne Porter's autobiographical "Pale Horse, Pale Rider" (1939).

Nell—A Shakespearean character in *Henry IV: Part I* and *Part II, Henry V,* and *The Merry Wives of Windsor,* Mistress Nell Quickly has bottomless energy but little sense. Charles Dickens's Nell Trent, known as "Little Nell" in *The Old Curiosity Shop* (1840), is delicate, too much so to endure.

Octavia—Though bearing a pretty-sounding name, Octavia is jilted. Mark Antony leaves her for Cleopatra, as described in William Shakespeare's *Antony and Cleopatra* (1607) and in John Dryden's *All for Love* (1678).

Olivia—Olivia is the monied young countess, desired by Orsino, who instead has a yen for his page, Cesario (who is really Viola), in William Shakespeare's *Twelfth Night* (1601).

Ophelia—Hamlet's good-looking but weak-minded love interest in William Shakespeare's *Hamlet* (1602) goes mad when her father, Polonius, dies.

Paulina—Paulina is Hermione's good friend, an aristocrat who brings about her resurrection in William Shakespeare's *The Winter's Tale* (1611).

Perdita—As she appears in William Shakespeare's *The Winter's Tale* (1611), Perdita is pretty and sweet with high born overtones though she is a poor country maid. Not surprisingly, it turns out that she is the misplaced princess of Sicily.

Portia—The ever so smart and inventive Portia masquerades as a male lawyer to save Antonio in William Shakespeare's *The Merchant of Venice* (1595). Portia, Brutus's wife in William Shakespeare's *Julius Caesar* (1599), fares less well and commits suicide. Portia Quayne, in *The Death of the Heart* (1938) by Elizabeth Bowen, becomes a realist when her pie in the sky plops.

Rosalynde (Rosalind)—*Rosalynde, Euphues' Golden Legacie* (1590) by Thomas Locke was the basis for William Shakespeare's *As You Like It* (1598). That courageous, witty Rosalind has a gift for bons mots and masquerade. She is Celia's great friend.

Sappho—Sappho, a remarkable real-life female poet of ancient Greece, threw herself into the sea when rejected by the youth Phaon. Find the story in *Sappho and Phaon*, plays by John Lyly (1594) and Percy MacKaye (1907).

Selene—This distant and unapproachable goddess each night escorted the moon across the heavens by chariot. Zeus put Endymion to sleep so he could dream of her forever. John Lyly wrote of it in *Endymion and the Man on the Moone* (1585).

Silvia—Silvia is the winsome daughter of the duke of Milan in William Shakespeare's *The Two Gentlemen of Verona* (1592).

Sofronia—Sofronia's lover, Olindo, offers to die in her stead. Authorities decide they should both die; however, Clorinda rescues them at the last moment in *Jerusalem Delivered* by Torquato Tasso (1581).

Thaisa—Pericles' wife, whom he wins through jousting, seems to die in childbirth. Happily, she turns up later as a priestess in William Shakespeare's *Pericles, Prince of Tyre* (1604).

Titania—This sexy and stubborn queen of the faeries in William Shakespeare's *A Midsummer Night's Dream* (1594) holds fast to her promise to raise a dead friend's child, which causes problems in her marriage. She appeared earlier in Ovid's *Metamorphoses* (first century A.D.).

Una—Una is Edmund Spenser's tribute to Queen Elizabeth and Protestantism in *The Faerie Queene* (1590–96). Heroine of the first book of the epic poem, the fair maiden represents truth. Author Nathaniel Hawthorne named his firstborn Una.

Viola—Sebastian's twin sister in William Shakespeare's love tangle *Twelfth Night* (1601), Viola is smitten with Orsino. Disguised as a man named

Cesario, she attracts Olivia, over whom Orsino is lovesick.

Virgilia—Virgilia is Coriolanus's gentle, compassionate wife in William Shakespeare's *Coriolanus* (1608).

Volumnia—She is Coriolanus's indomitable patrician mother in William Shakespeare's *Coriolanus* (1608).

Elizabethan Men's Names

Alexander (Alex, Alec, Alexey)—Alexander the Great, a Macedonian leader of tremendous prowess and charisma, conqueror of the civilized world in the fourth century B.C., is the subject of John Lyly's *Alexander and Campaspe* (1581) and a tragedy by Racine, *Alexandre le Grand* (1665). Alexei Vronsky, a rich and good-looking officer, is not to be hemmed in by love. Alexei Karenin is a smart austere coward. Both men are in *Anna Karenina* (1876) by Leo Tolstoy. Lecherous trouble causer Alec d'Urberville knocks up *Tess of the D'Urbervilles* (1891) by Thomas Hardy. Their child, whom Tess has the prescience to name Sorrow, dies—as does Alec, at Tess's hands.

Angelo—Shakepeare's Angelo the goldsmith is a good fellow in his *A Comedy of Errors* (1594), but the Angelo in his *Measure for Measure* (1604) is quite different. Rigid morality masks the vicious nature of this lord deputy.

Antonio—The dejected merchant is a good friend to Bassanio in William Shakespeare's *The Merchant of Venice* (1596). Antonio is the underhanded sibling who causes Prospero's banishment in *The Tempest* (1611). Antonio is also Rudolf A. Anaya's bright and questioning protagonist who so vividly captures the experience of growing up Chicano in *Bless Me, Ultima* (1992).

Antony (Anthony)—Antony in William Shakespeare's *Julius Caesar* (1599) feels torn in his allegiance to Caesar, but comes forward bravely after Caesar's death to unite forces against Brutus. William Shakespeare's *Antony and Cleopatra* finds the general in the autumn of his glory (1606). *All for Love* by John Dryden (1678) recounts the battle for Antony's soul between assorted women and his general. English spy and art historian Sir Anthony Blunt is John Banville's hero in *The Untouchable* (1997).

Artegal—Artegal represents justice in Edmund Spenser's *The Faerie Queen* (1590–96).

Astrophel—Astrophel is a man who loves too late from *Astrophel and Stella,* a sonnet series by Sir Philip Sidney (1591) celebrating a hopeless love affair. "Astrophel" is also the title of a poem Edmund Spenser wrote (1586) to commemorate Sidney on his death.

Bajazet—Bajazet is Tamburlaine's fiercest opponent in Christopher Marlowe's *Tamburlaine the Great* (1590). He is also a seventeenth-century prisoner in Constantinople in Jean Racine's *Bajazet* (1672), which depicts the numerous deaths that result from the sultana Roxane's unrequited love.

Balthazar—Balthazar is Don Pedro's servant in William Shakespeare's *Much Ado About Nothing* (1598) and a merchant in his *Comedy of Errors* (1594). In *Journey to the End of Night* (1932) by Louis-Ferdinand Céline, Balthazar is a character most noted for his "terrific penis." The Jewish doctor Balthazar is the head of the cabal in Lawrence Durrell's *Balthazar* (1958), one of *The Alexandria Quartet* novels. A historian, he deals in arcane mysterious black magic.

Banquo—Banquo is the deceased Scottish thane of the highest moral caliber whose spirit later plagues William Shakespeare's *Macbeth* (1606).

Bassanio—Penniless but inventive, he is Portia's ardent suitor, in love with both her and her money in William Shakespeare's *The Merchant of Venice* (1596).

Bassanius—Bassanius is Lavinia's love in William Shakespeare's *Titus Andronicus* (1590), too good to survive the gruesome events.

Benedick—William Shakespeare's cocky, confirmed bachelor is both no match and the ideal match for Beatrice in *Much Ado About Nothing* (1598).

Benvolio—Romeo's good-tempered cousin William Shakespeare's *Romeo and Juliet* (1596) is loyal but not as fiery as Mercutio.

Bertram—Although a likable chap, Bertram mistreats Helena in William Shakespeare's *All's Well That Ends Well* (1610). That she forgives him ruins the play for many people. Edmund Bertram in Jane Austen's *Mansfield Park* (1814) takes the whole book to come to his senses.

Caesar—William Shakespeare's *Julius Caesar* (1599) is an admirable and triumphant leader who disregards threats against him, as he is convinced of his invincibility.

Calidore—Calidore represents courtesy in Edmund Spenser's *The Faerie Queen* (1590–96)

Claudio—In William Shakespeare's *Measure for Measure* (1604), Isabella's brother Claudio follows his heart rather than his spiritual beliefs. Claudio is also a good-looking Florentine soldier in Shakespeare's *Much Ado About Nothing* (1598); he immediately becomes infatuated with Hero but has to wrestle with his suspicious nature. Everyone else *jests* with his suspicious nature.

Colin—Colin Clout, "shepherd of the ocean," is Edmund Spenser's allegorical Sir Walter Raleigh in *Colin Clout's Come Home Again* (1595). Colin is a sickly whiner in Francis Hodgson Burnett's *Secret Garden* (1911) until transformed by fresh air into a decent chap.

Coriolanus—This brave, fierce warrior is also an elitist, and not particularly popular, in William Shakespeare's *Coriolanus* (1608).

Cymbeline—This good and gracious king of Britain is misled by his wicked wife in William Shakespeare's *Cymbeline* (1609).

Demetrius—Demetrius is a rake who wants Hermia for her money but is willing to have a fling with Helena in the meantime in William Shakespeare's *A Midsummer Night's Dream* (1594). Hermia throws him over for Lysander.

Duncan—Duncan is the good and beloved king of Scotland, murdered by William Shakespeare's *Macbeth* (1606).

Edgar—In William Shakespeare's *King Lear* (1605), Edgar is the earl of Gloucester's legitimate son, disinherited due to his bastard brother's falsehoods and treachery.

Edmund (Edmond)—In William Shakespeare's *King Lear* (1605), Edmund is the earl of Gloucester's treacherous illegitimate son. Edmund, duke of York, is a far more loyal figure in Shakespeare's *Richard II* (1595). Fanny Price's beloved cleric Edmund finally comes to his senses in Jane Austen's *Mansfield Park* (1813). Daring, dark, and mysterious, Edmond Dantès is the protagonist of *The Count of Monte Cristo* by Alexandre Dumas (1844). Edmund Scrubbs, "who almost deserves his name," comes around to being a better sort of boy in C. S. Lewis's *The Chronicles of Narnia* (1950–56).

Endymion—The gods keep this mythical young man forever young with perpetual slumber, during which he dreams of his beloved moon goddess, Selene. John Lyly wrote *Endymion and the Man on the Moone* (1585). John Keats wrote a narrative poem *Endymion* (1818) and dedicated it to young Thomas Chatterton, a poet who committed suicide at age eighteen.

Euphues—John Lyly wrote two works on *Euphues* (1578–80) featuring his high wit and overly ornate manner of speech. Bombastic expression like this is now known as "euphuistic."

Faust—Faust is a German magician and fortune-teller who sells his soul to the devil, Mephistopheles (not a good name for a child), in exchange for supernatural powers. In Christopher Marlowe's *The Tragical History of Doctor Faustus* (uncertain, 1589–1604) this turns out poorly, but in Johann Wolfgang von Goethe's nineteenth-century version, *Faust,* the doctor is motivated by a genuine desire to increase his knowledge and does not go to hell after all. Thomas Mann's *Doktor Faustus* (1947) suggests that the human condition and its degradation can subvert untrammeled creative passion.

Ferdinand—In William Shakespeare's *Love's Labour's Lost* (1598), this king of Navarre commits to cultivating arts and intellect in lieu of pursuing earthly pleasures. Ferdinand is also a prince who falls desperately and immediately in love with Miranda in Shakespeare's *The Tempest* (1611).

Feste—Feste is Olivia's clown in William Shakespeare's *Twelfth Night* (1601).

Fleance—Fleance, Banquo's son in William Shakespeare's *Macbeth* (1606), escapes to Wales and busily produces children to become heirs to the House of Stuart, just as the "double toil and trouble" witches predicted he would.

Florizel—Polixenes' son, prince of Bohemia, is particularly dashing as he carries off Perdita in William Shakespeare's *The Winter's Tale* (1611).

Fortinbras—Fortinbras is the prince of Norway in William Shakespeare's *Hamlet* (1602), his decisive energetic nature in direct contrast to Hamlet's ambivalence.

George—The original George slays the dragon, expressing the triumph of the Christian hero over Satan. The patron saint of England, he is the Red Cross Knight in Edmund Spenser's *The Faerie Queen* (1590–96). Thomas Percy likewise saluted George in *Reliques of Ancient English Poetry* (1765). Centuries later, E. M. Forster conceived the unrestrained George Emerson as a natural and passionate bourgeois in *A Room with a View* (1908). H. G. Wells's character George Ponderevo in *Tono-Bungay* (1909), like Wells himself, begins with nothing and finds a way to profit through science. Sherwood Anderson's cub reporter George Willard tries to buck the provincial nature of *Winesburg, Ohio* (1919), a process through which he matures. Middle-class George Babbitt's halfhearted efforts to rise above his mediocrity are the subject of Sinclair Lewis's *Babbitt* (1922). Then there is John Steinbeck's wiry George Milton, whose loving defense of his friend Lenny requires that he shoot him dead in *Of Mice and Men* (1937). John P. Marquand paid homage to a most traditional Bostonian in *The Late George Apley* (1937). Thornton Wilder's George Gibbs, in his play *Our Town* (1938), is a decent chap and high-school baseball hero. George Webber, Thomas Wolfe's autobiographical hero in *The Web and the Rock* (1939) and *You Can't Go Home Again* (1940), explores opportunity and looks for meaning in New York and abroad. George Smiley, venerable and adept, is a British secret service agent in John le Carré's *The Spy Who Came In from the Cold* (1963).

Godfrey (Goffredo)—Godfrey, a tremendously romantic character, is the devout and infallible crusader hero of *Jerusalem Delivered* by Torquato Tasso (1581). Divinely called to his quests, he overcomes every danger.

Guyon—In Edmund Spenser's *The Faerie Queen* (1590–96), Guyon represents Temperance, as contrasted with Acrasia (Intemperance).

Hamlet—This indecisive and overly reflective young prince is given to passionate outbursts in William Shakespeare's *Hamlet* (1602).

Helicanus—Helicanus is Pericles' loyal and unambitious counselor throughout William Shakespeare's *Pericles, Prince of Tyre* (1604).

Henry—Kings, navigators, rich men, etc., Henrys are ubiquitous. Practically everyone in William Shake-

speare's *Henry IV: Part I* (1596) is named Henry.
Henry IV is the able but anxious king. His son Henry
V, Prince Hal, is entirely irresponsible until *Henry
IV: Part II*, during which he undergoes a transfor-
mation and emerges a ready king. And Henry Percy,
known as "Hotspur," is as widely respected as
Prince Hal is scorned. In *Henry V* (1599), Prince
Hal comes out of his wretched chrysalis and be-
comes a brave and majestic leader. In Shakespeare's
Richard II (1595), Henry Bolingbroke, duke of Her-
ford, has "king" written all over him as he usurps
the throne. Split personality is the type engendered
by Henry Jekyll of Robert Louis Stevenson's *Dr.
Jekyll and Mr. Hyde*, 1883. Henry Fleming struggles against his fear during the Civil War in Stephen
Crane's *The Red Badge of Courage* (1895). "John
Henry" is a prodigiously strong black railroad
worker on a par with Pecos Bill and Paul Bunyan.
William Faulkner's Henry Sutpen in *Absalom,
Absalom!* (1936) is a forceful idealist but not particularly shrewd. Lawyer Henry Drummond, the
Clarence Darrow character in Jerome Lawrence's
Inherit the Wind (1955), passionately defends the
evolutionist schoolteacher. George Bernard Shaw's
character Henry Higgins, an exacting and curmud-
geonly professor of phonetics, plays the Pygmalion
role in *Pygmalion* (1913), the basis for the musical
My Fair Lady.

Horatio—Horatio is Hamlet's good and loyal friend
in William Shakespeare's *Hamlet* (1602). In the
nineteenth century, Horatio Alger wrote stories

about boys who begin impoverished and end wealthy through virtuous behavior. His name has come to represent such figures. In *Captain Horatio Hornblower* (1937) by C. S. Forester, the retiring Horatio, rippling with muscles and brave, is at the helm of the *Lydia*.

Hugh—The robust former commander of crusading French soldiers, Hugh appears to Godfrey in a vision in *Jerusalem Delivered* by Torquato Tasso (1581). In James Hilton's *Lost Horizon* (1933), charismatic and brilliant Hugh Conway becomes a shoo-in for the High Lama position in Shangri-la.

John—Since his head's appearance on a platter, a result of the machinations of Salomé in the New Testament, John is everywhere. William Shakespeare's *King John* (1596) is a simpering, ineffectual leader who is insensitive to his people and steals from the clergy. Sir John Falstaff, one of Shakespeare's most endearing creations, is a colossal blowhard and voluptuary who appears in *Henry IV, Part I* and *Part II* (1596), as well as *The Merry Wives of Windsor* (1596). Thanks to John Arbuthnot's *History of John Bull* (1712), bighearted, stubborn "John Bull" came to symbolize England. Neither John Willoughby nor John Dashwood in Jane Austen's *Sense and Sensibility* (1811) is of a namesake caliber, though John Harmon, of Charles Dickens's *Our Mutual Friend* (1864), is a man "of spirit and resource." Little John bests Robin Hood, then swears to be Hood's bouncer; he appears in many accounts, including Sir Walter Scott's *The Talisman* (1825). John Alden speaks to Priscilla Mullins for the captain in Henry Wadsworth Longfellow's *The Courtship of Miles Standish* (1858) and she falls in love with Alden instead. Then there are the mutinous, charismatic, and deceitful Long John Silver in Robert Louis Stevenson's *Treasure Island* (1883) and trouble causer John Claggart in Herman Melville's *Billy Budd* (1901). John Thornton is the long-awaited kind master of Buck the dog in Jack London's *The Call of the Wild* (1903). There's folk hero Johnny Appleseed, *né* John Chapman, about whom Vachel Lindsay wrote a long poem, "In Praise of Johnny Appleseed" (1923). Stephen Vincent Benét immortalized the valorous raid on Harper's Ferry during the American Civil War in "John Brown's Body" (1928). In Ford Madox Ford's *Good Soldier* (1915), ineffectual John Dowell struggles to comprehend the behavior of his wife and dearest friends. Ayn Rand's John Galt in *Atlas Shrugged* (1957), constantly mentioned yet nowhere to be found, epitomizes man's noblest and most heroic qualities, just as elusive as he is. Johnny is Stephen King's maniacal family man in *The Shining* (1977).

Laurence (Lawrence)—Laurence is the sweet-tempered and sympathetic friar who counsels the star-crossed lovers in William Shakespeare's *Romeo and Juliet* (1596). Lawrence is also the last name of the celebrated T. E. Lawrence, Lawrence of Arabia, the most-written-about English soldier of World War I. Lawrence had a huge following; he later sought obscurity.

Leander—Leander was a legendary Greek swimmer who stroked across the Hellespont every night to visit his lover, the priestess Hero, until he drowned in a storm. Christopher Marlowe wrote an account of this myth, *Hero and Leander,* completed by George Chapman after Marlowe's death (1593).

Leontes—Leontes, the king of Sicily, though well intended, mistrusts his wife and friend, effectively causing the plot problems of William Shakespeare's *The Winter's Tale* (1611).

Lucius—Lucius is Titus's son and the sole survivor of William Shakespeare's bloody *Titus Andronicus* (1590) who after relinquishing his ferocious ways becomes emperor in the end.

Lysander—A good and virtuous bearer of flowers and performer of serenades, Lysander is unstoppable in his love for Hermia in William Shakespeare's *A Midsummer Night's Dream* (1594).

Menenius—Menenius is the quick-witted and conciliatory friend to William Shakespeare's *Coriolanus* (1608).

Mercutio—Romeo's brave, witty, and pugnacious comrade in William Shakespeare's *Romeo and Juliet* (1596).

Oberon—Oberon, the forceful and unbending king of the faeries in William Shakespeare's *A Midsummer Night's Dream* (1594), seems given to pettiness in his dealings with his queen. Oberon appeared earlier in *Huon de Bordeaux* (prose fiction of the fifteenth century) as the son of Morgan le Fay and Julius Caesar.

Octavius—Octavius is the calculating and purposeful emperor of Rome whose manipulations so daunt the protagonists of *Antony and Cleopatra* by William Shakespeare (1607). His appearance in Shakespeare's *Julius Caesar* (1599) foretells his willfulness.

Olindo—Sofronia's lover, Olindo offers to die for her at the stake. Authorities decide they should both die; however, Clorinda rescues them at the last moment in *Jerusalem Delivered* by Torquato Tasso (1581).

Orsino—Orsino is William Shakespeare's powerful and sentimental duke in *Twelfth Night* (1601).

Othello—Othello is a Moorish general of "free and open nature" whom Iago manipulates into a frenzy of distrust in William Shakespeare's *Othello* (1604).

Ottone—Ottone is one of the most dauntless knights of *Jerusalem Delivered* by Torquato Tasso (1581). He is eventually challenged and slain by Argante.

Panurge—Panurge is the cunning but charismatic rogue in François Rabelais's *Gargantua and Pantagruel* (1532).

Pedro—Don Pedro is Hero's doubtful suitor in William Shakespeare's *Much Ado About Nothing*

(1598). In the first book to emerge from the Spanish Americas, *The Itching Parrot* (1816) by Fernández de Lizardi, Pedro Sarmiento is a young rascal who turns respectable after many failed professions. Lady Brett has a fling with the young impressionable Pedro Romero, a gifted bullfighter, in Ernest Hemingway's *The Sun Also Rises* (1926).

Pericles—This classic hero endures all and, uncomplainingly, just keeps enduring, in William Shakespeare's comedy-romance *Pericles, Prince of Tyre* (1604).

Petruchio—This intrepid boisterous hulk takes on *The Taming of the Shrew* by William Shakespeare (1593) and does so.

Philip—This is the well-intentioned king of France in William Shakespeare's *King John* (1596) whose support for John's rival is undone as his soldiers are continually lost at sea. Philip "Pip" Pirrup, hero of Charles Dickens's *Great Expectations* (1860) and a good and decent lad, spends the novel trying to become a gentleman so as to merit his promised inheritance of unknown origin. W. Somerset Maugham's character Philip Carey is a thoughtful, sensitive young man who aspires to become an artist. He is impaired by a clubfoot. Artist and eager amateur detective Philip Trent weighs solutions to a murder in *Trent's Last Case* (1912) by E. C. Bentley. Principled detective Philip Marlowe has great moxie in *The Big Sleep* (1939) and other of Raymond Chandler's novels.

Polixenes—Polixenes is Leontes's good friend, whom Leontes unjustly accuses of adultery in William Shakespeare's *The Winter's Tale* (1611).

Posthumus—A gentleman of uncertain birth, Posthumus loves Imogen deeply but nevertheless distrusts her in William Shakespeare's *Cymbeline* (1609). Doubling the trouble, his name sounds like an afterthought.

Prospero—Prospero is a duke who devotes his marvelous mind to tasks of magic in William Shakespeare's *The Tempest* (1611).

Quixote—Noble but bony old knight of Miguel de Cervantes's *Don Quixote de la Mancha* (1605) who pursues a mad and wildly inventive chivalric lifestyle.

Ralph—*Ralph Roister Doister* (1553) by Nicholas Udall concerns a loud, lumbering man who clumsily persists in his efforts to secure a widow's affections.

Richard—Richards are generally upstanding characters. William Shakespeare's *Richard II* (1595), though deeply eloquent, just wears king's clothes without *being* a king in his soul. Shakespeare's *Richard III* (1595) is sadistic and power-hungry in the classic Machiavellian tradition. Richard the Lion-hearted, king of England, figures in Sir Walter Scott's historical novels of the early nineteenth century. Richard Saunders was Benjamin Franklin's *nom de plume* for *Poor Richard's Almanac* (1732–

57). Richard (Dick) Swiveller in Charles Dickens's *Old Curiosity Shop* (1840) is a grimy and wrinkled hummer of baleful melodies. George Meredith's 1859 novel, *The Ordeal of Richard Feverel,* was banned as immoral; this Richard is home-schooled, with the fairer sex kept at bay, and all pandemonium breaks loose when he finds out what he's been missing. Schoolmaster Richard Phillotson tries to direct Jude's academic pursuits in *Jude the Obscure* by Thomas Hardy (1895). Richard Carvel is hero of Winston Churchill's novel by the same name (1899), about Richard's adventures aboard a slaver during the American Revolution. Richard Hannay, a mining engineer who uncovers a spy ring, prevents an invasion of Britain in John Buchan's *The Thirty-nine Steps* (1915).

Romeo—The quintessential romantic type, he has a gift for artful expression in William Shakespeare's *Romeo and Juliet* (1596).

Sebastian—Viola's twin brother eventually reappears to win Olivia, whom Viola, dressed as a man, has unintentionally courted in William Shakespeare's *Twelfth Night* (1601).

Tamburlaine (Tamerlane, Timor i Leng)—Tamburlaine is Genghis Khan's great-great-grandson and cut from the same cloth. In Christopher Marlowe's *Tamburlaine the Great* (1590), he appears as a vicious and bloodthirsty scourge. However, in Nicholas Rowe's *Tamerlane* (1702), he is a less rambunctious, more philosophical type.

Tancred—Tancred is a heroic crusader who took part in the siege of Jerusalem. He falls in love with an Ethiopian warrior princess whom he unintentionally wounds mortally in *Jerusalem Delivered* by Torquato Tasso (1581). In Benjamin Disraeli's novel *Tancred, or The New Crusade* (1847), he is a high-minded aristocrat who leaves London to explore the Orient.

Toby—This name seems to typify good-natured and heavy-drinking types such as Sir Toby Belch in William Shakespeare's *Twelfth Night* (1601).

Triamond—Sir Triamond is a knight representing friendship in Edmund Spenser's *The Faerie Queen* (1590–96).

Valentine—In William Shakespeare's *Two Gentlemen of Verona* (1592), the valorous and generous Valentine is Proteus' rival for the hand of Silvia. Valentines have had a resurgence in twentieth-century science fiction. Valentine Michael Smith, an earthling raised by Martians, returns to Earth in Robert Heinlein's *Stranger in a Strange Land* (1961). He starts a successful religion and is killed, like other messiahs before him. Author Robert Silverberg created Prince Valentine Pontifex to live on the giant world of Majipoor in *Lord Valentine's Castle* (1980) and others of the Majipoor series. Though starting off as a juggler, Valentine learns that his mind has been wiped by the shape-shifters. They have replaced him as lord of the planet. Valentine Wiggin appears in Orson

Scott Card's *Ender's Game* (1984) and others of the series. As Ender Wiggin's sister and a handy computer support person, he battles a hostile government.

RECLAIMING CLASSICISM:

Neoclassic Names (from the 1620s through the eighteenth century)

*B*Y the late seventeenth century, literary characters found themselves much more democratic in their beliefs and consequently less reverential toward monarchs. Religious controversy charged literature with fervor. Scientific discovery brought about the Age of Reason, favoring earlier models established by Greeks and Romans. Hence, this time frame is referred to as the "neoclassic period." These trends made room for satire, literature about society, and, indeed, the birth of the modern novel, which the increasing number of readers readily welcomed. Much of the literature of this period emphasized religious, social, and political criticism.

Neoclassic Women's Names

Agnès (Agnes)—The name of Molière's captivating innocent in *L'École des Femmes* (1662) has become synonymous with naïveté. Agnes is also a sad and solitary governess in Anne Brontë's *Agnes Grey* (1847).

Althea—Althea means "wholesome" in Greek. She is the wife of Oeneus, the first man to cultivate grapes. An Althea was the inspiration for a seventeenth-century poem by Edmund Waller, written in prison.

Amelia (Amélie)—Amélie is Cinna's beloved; wanting to avenge her father's death, she conspires with Cinna to kill the emperor Augustus in Pierre Corneille's *Cinna* (1640). Henry Fielding's *Amelia* (1751) is a virtuous, forgiving, and long-suffering heroine who "stands by her guy," even though he spends most of the book behind bars.

Annabella—Beautiful, incestuous Annabella is ultimately dead, as are several other characters in John Ford's *'Tis Pity She's a Whore* (1627).

Anthea—From a Greek word meaning "flowery," Anthea is the inspiration for a poem by seventeenth-century poet Robert Herrick: "thou art my life, my love, my heart, the very eyes of me; and hast command of everypart, to live and die for thee."

Arabella—The real life Arabella Fermor's tendril moved Alexander Pope to compose *The Rape of the Lock* (1712). (The author changed her name to "Belinda.") In *Jude the Obscure* (1895) by Thomas Hardy, another Arabella is a bit of a floozy with an insatiable penchant for men and drink.

Aretina—Aretina is a wife who cannot control her purse strings in James Shirley's *The Lady of Pleasure* (1635).

Bathsheba—In the Bible, David absconds with Uriah's wife, Bathsheba. In John Dryden's political satire, *Absalom and Achitophel* (1681), Bathsheba represents Louise Kerouatte, the duchess of Portsmouth, a favorite of Charles II. Later she is the beautiful, impetuous heroine of Thomas Hardy's *Far from the Madding Crowd* (1874).

Belinda—Belinda's snipped lock is a "triumph in insignificance" in Alexander Pope's satirical poem *The Rape of the Lock* (1712).

Bérénice—She is the heroine and title of dueling plays by Jean Racine and Pierre Corneille (1670 and 1672). Both concern the thwarted love of a Palestinian queen and the Roman emperor Titus. Another Berenice, an epileptic with a nice set of pearly-whites, is in Edgar Allan Poe's tale of the same name (1835).

Camille (Camilla)—In Pierre Corneille's play *Horace* (1640), Camille is Horace's sister. When Horace kills her fiancé, Camille curses Rome, whereupon Horace slays her, too. Camilla is a young innocent introduced into society, a romantic heroine from the imagination of Fanny Burney in a book of the same name (1796). The heroine of *La Dame aux Camélias* (1852) of Alexandre Dumas, *fils,* stunning courtesan Marguerite Gauthier, is known in America as Camille. She is a woman with no gift for self-preservation but a great gift for love.

Celestina—In James Shirley's *The Lady of Pleasure* (1635), Celestina is an exceptionally appealing widow.

Célimène—She is a frivolous little tease in Molière's *The Misanthrope* (1666).

Charlotte—Charlotte Temple, one of the most popular heroines of her era, appears in a book of the same name by Susanna Rowson (1791). Young and thoughtful, she is based on a real woman named Charlotte Stanley. Thomas Mann invents the simple but good Lotte in his *The Beloved Returns* (1939). Charlotte is also Wilbur's motherly mentor in E. B. White's *Charlotte's Web* (1952).

Clarissa (Clarisse)—In Madeleine de Scudéry's *Clélie* (1654–60), Clarisse is a portrait of the French demimondaine, Anne Lenclos. Poor Clarissa, in the voluminous *Clarissa Harlowe* by Samuel Richardson (1747–48), has the highest moral standards; at first she is thwarted by her family and then by the man she loves. Clarissa Dalloway, in the novel *Mrs. Dalloway* (1925) by Virginia Woolf, reflects on her life as she prepares for a party. In Ray Bradbury's *Fahrenheit 451,* a young Clarisse, though an outcast, recognizes life's beauty; she sniffs Montag's clothes and tells him his fate.

Cloelia—According to legend, Cloelia is a brave hostage who escapes the Etruscans by swimming across the Tiber. Madeleine de Scudéry took this romance and expanded it in *Clélie* (1654–60). Clélie swims the Tiber, after ten volumes, to reunite with her lover, Aronce.

Dorinda—Dorinda is Lady Bountiful's captivating daughter in *The Beaux' Stratagem,* a comedy by George Farquhar (1707).

Dorothea—*The Virgin Martyr* (1622) by Philip Massinger retells the story of the rose-bearing Dorothea, who, after dying, sends fruit and apples, borne by an angel, to her judge.

Eliante—She is the kindest and best of women in Molière's *The Misanthrope* (1666).

Elise—Elise is the lovely daughter of the niggardly Harpagon in Molière's *The Miser* (1668).

Esther—Esther was a beautiful, brave storyteller in the Old Testament and in Jean Racine's play *Esther* (1689). Dear, good Esther Summerson is in Charles Dickens's *Bleak House* (1852). In George Eliot's *Felix Holt, the Radical* (1866), an Esther is wooed by Felix and his rival; she realizes her true affections when Felix is in trouble. Henry Adams's *Esther Dudley* (1884) is an artist who falls in love with a clergyman whom she later rejects because of his beliefs. A resourceful Esther Jack appears in Thomas Wolfe's *The Web and the Rock* (1939) and *You Can't Go Home Again* (1940). In *The Bell Jar* (1963), Sylvia Plath's Esther Greenwood is a bright young woman driven mad in ruminations about sex and the company of men.

Eve—The original woman has a lust for autumn fruit in John Milton's *Paradise Lost* (1667).

Evelina—A young innocent introduced into society, Evelina is a heroine from the imagination of Fanny Burney in a book of the same name (1778). She seeks love and her heritage.

Glumdalclitch—This is a girl, as tall as a building, whom Gulliver befriends in Jonathan Swift's *Gulliver's Travels,* published in 1726.

Héloïse (Eloise, Eloisa)—Héloïse and Pierre Abelard were actual lovers of the Middle Ages, tragically separated. Their exchange of correspondence made them famous, as celebrated in Alexander Pope's *Eloisa to Abelard* (1717). They were exhumed and reburied in the same grave in 1817. In *Eloise* (1952) by Hilary Knight, an even more avant-garde Eloise is a delightful imp who lives at and terrorizes the Plaza Hotel in Manhattan. She just loves room service.

Justine—*Justine* (1791) is a novel about a woman sexually violated by the Marquis de Sade. Justine is also the mysterious, irresistible, and gunrunning heroine of *Justine* (1957) and other volumes of Lawrence Durrell's *The Alexandria Quartet*.

Lucasta—Poet Richard Lovelace wrote the lines "I could not love thee, dear so much, lov'd I not Honour more" as he sets out for war in "To Lucasta" (1649).

Lucinde—Lucinde was the original anorexic, the heroine of Molière's *L'Amour Medecin* and *Le Mede-*

cin Malgré Lui (1665) who can only be cured by true love.

Manon—Manon Lescaut is a persuasive lower-class woman who drives her lover into the poorhouse, in the Abbé Prévost's novel *Manon Lescaut* (1771).

Margery—Margery has a paranoid husband named Pinchwife, whose suspicions that she is untrue drive her to infidelity, in William Wycherley's *The Country Wife* (1675).

Mathilda—Mathilda is a noblewoman who plays out a diabolical mission to corrupt Ambrosio, an abbot in Matthew Gregory Lewis's *The Monk* (1795).

Mignon—In Johann Wolfgang von Goethe's *Wilhelm Meister* (1795), Mignon is an adolescent performer who lashes her hopes to Wilhelm.

Millanant—She is the clever and sophisticated heroine of William Congreve's *The Way of the World* (1700).

Moll—The delightful London prostitute and heroine of Daniel Defoe's *The Fortunes and Misfortunes of Moll Flanders* (1722) who, though a consummate thief, eventually escapes her life of vice. Molly Bloom is Leopold's pleasure-sensitive wife in James Joyce's *Ulysses* (1922). She is open and approachable. This leads her to embrace life as it occurs, in quantities beyond what her husband will allow himself.

Oenone—Poor Oenone, playing the part of a nurse, comes to a sorry ending in Jean Racine's *Phèdre*

(1677). Oenone is also a lovely nymph of Mount Ida, married to Paris. He deserts her for Helen, as mournfully described in a poem by Alfred, Lord Tennyson, "Oenone" (1832).

Pamela—Samuel Richardson's heroine in *Pamela, or Virtue Rewarded* (1742) is a chaste and willful country girl who sets her sights on a rich husband and sticks to them.

Sophie—The girl slated to marry Jean-Jacques Rousseau's Emile. The emphasis of Sophie's education was on pleasing men; however, her infidelity destroys her marriage in *Emile and Sophie* (1762).

Stella—Stella is Jonathan Swift's name for Esther Johnson, the most important woman of his life, from *Journal to Stella*, commenced in 1710. In Tennessee Williams's *A Streetcar Named Desire* (1947), Stella is Blanche's married and more conventional sister. In Bernard Malamud's "The Magic Barrel" (1958), Leo Finkle falls in love with the matchmaker's daughter, Stella, when he sees her photograph.

Tabitha—Husband-hungry Tabitha Bramble is Matthew Bramble's sister in Tobias George Smollett's *The Expedition of Humphrey Clinker* (1771). She is a notoriously poor speller.

Undine (Ondine)—She a water nymph whose love for a knight ends tragically in Friedrich von Fouqué's *Undine* (1811) and Jean Giraudoux's *Ondine* (1939).

Winifred—The appealing Winifred Jenkins is Matthew Bramble's maid in Tobias George Smollett's *The Expedition of Humphrey Clinker* (1771).

Neoclassic Men's Names

Abelard—Theologian Peter Abelard was famously in love with Héloïse. Their devotion lives on from their letters of the twelfth century. These classics of romantic correspondence were the subject of Alexander Pope's *Eloisa to Abelard* (1717). Héloïse's uncle had Abelard castrated. His time thus freed up, Abelard entered a monastery, where he remained a forceful philosopher.

Adam—The original man was minus a rib, God having used it to craft Eve, whom neither Adam nor God could control. Adam appears often, early on in John Milton's *Paradise Lost* (1667). Then there is George Eliot's *Adam Bede* (1859), whose lofty values are strained. Dr. Adam Stanton, an essentially good man, so regrets Willie Starks's existence that he assassinates him, not a moment too soon, in Robert Penn Warren's *All the King's Men* (1946). Cuckolded Adam Trask raises two boys on his own in John Steinbeck's *East of Eden* (1952). Adam Dalgliesh is P. D. James's creation, a detective inspector with acutely refined deductive skills in her mysteries (1966–72).

Alceste—Alceste, essentially a decent type, forswears hypocrisy in Molière's *The Misanthrope* (1666) and ends up alone and thoroughly depressed.

Ambrosio—This reverent abbot is corrupted by Mathilda in Matthew Gregory Lewis's *The Monk* (1795).

Arnolphe—Molière's wealthy didact fancies himself an apt teacher for wives in *L'École des Femmes* (1662).

Astrolabe—Astrolabe was Héloïse and Abelard's love child, named after a tool used to measure the heavens. Astrolabe means "to seize the stars." Héloïse and Abélard's exchange of letters made them

Molière (1622–73), whose given name was Jean-Baptiste Poquelin, devoted himself to the theater from an early age. His troupe, the Illustre Théâtre, struggled in Paris then played in the provinces for thirteen years before returning to Paris triumphant. Molière, the comic genius of his time, was at once dramatist, actor, producer, and director. His farces boldly satirized the vacuity and hypocrisy he saw around him. Though Molière took chances by spoofing the Church and the materialistic bourgeoisie, and was often criticized for tastelessness, his work was immensely popular under patronage to Louis XIV at the Palais Royal. It is still considered the apogee of French comedy. Ironically, he collapsed onstage in his play The Imaginary Invalid and died a few hours later.

famous, as celebrated in Alexander Pope's *Eloisa to Abélard* (1717).

Beelzebub—Not until the New Testament was Beelzebub more than an oracular genius with a gift for controlling flies and, therefore, the diseases they carry. There and in *Paradise Lost* by John Milton (1667) he becomes Satan's flunky.

Candide—Candide is the calamity-prone but indefatigable hero of Voltaire's *Candide* (1759) whose misadventures conclude on a farm with his best friend and original love. Unfortunately, by that time he is thoroughly tired of them.

Charles—The sweet but impractical Dr. Charles Primrose is the engaging subject of Oliver Goldsmith's *Vicar of Wakefield* (1766). Primrose maintains his kindly disposition in spite of the corruption around him. The bright, droll Charles II, Stuart king of England, is featured in Sir Walter Scott's *Peveril of the Peak* (1822). Charles Cheerble is the stout and good-natured brother of Ned (Edwin) in Charles Dickens's *Nicholas Nickleby* (1838). Charles Swann is the narrator's part-Jewish neighbor who travels in elegant circles in Marcel Proust's *Swann's Way* (1913). Charles Bon is a sophisticated young student whose prospects are compromised more by the Sutpens than by his Negro blood in William Faulkner's *Absalom, Absalom!* (1936). Charles Ryder in Evelyn Waugh's *Brideshead Revisited* (1945) is an architectural painter who finds, unhappily, that he married the wrong sister.

Cinna—Cinna, an ambitious Roman, is greatly in love
with Amélie in Pierre Corneille's *Cinna* (1640).

Cophetua—Cophetua is an immensely affluent African king who falls in love with Penelophon in Thomas Percy's *Reliques* (1765) and Alfred, Lord
Tennyson's "The Beggar-Maid" (1885).

Emile—Jean-Jacques Rousseau's creation of 1762,
Emile is a boy brought up according to the principles of nature.

Friday—Friday is a grateful young Caribbean whom
the hero saves from cannibals in *Robinson Crusoe*
(1719) by Daniel Defoe. Friday becomes Robinson's loyal servant.

Gabriel—Gabriel, with his golden locks and mighty
wings, is a prince among archangels, always relay-
ing surprising news, ever ready to blow the horn on
Judgment Day. He appears in John Milton's *Paradise Lost* (1667) as chief guardian of Paradise. Ga-
briels are frequent and diverse throughout history.
Quiet and capable hero Gabriel Oak brings all
pieces together in Thomas Hardy's *Far from the
Madding Crowd* (1874). Henry Wadsworth Longfellow composed *Evangeline, A Tale of Acadia*
about Evangeline Bellefontaine and Gabriel Lajeunesse, two lovers put asunder by the British invasion
of Nova Scotia (1847). They don't reunite until Gabriel is on his deathbed. Another Gabriel, low-
spirited Gabriel Conroy, appears in James Joyce's
"The Dead" (1914).

Gulliver—Lemuel Gulliver is an English surgeon, sailor, and hero of Jonathan Swift's *Gulliver's Travels* (1726). The peripatetic Gulliver speaks several languages. His adventures satirize European governments of Swift's era, the early eighteenth century. Alfred Bester named his enhanced human agent Gully Foyle in the classic space story "Stars My Destination" (1956).

Harley—Harley is a wistful and sensitive good man in Henry Mackenzie's *The Man of Feeling* (1771).

Horace—Horace, though originally a fine Roman poet and satirist, makes an enthusiastic suitor to Agnès in Molière's *L'Ecole des Femmes* (1662). He is also the hotheaded vengeful hero of a tragedy, *Horace,* by Pierre Corneille (1640).

Humphrey—Humphrey is an unassuming servant who becomes a preacher in Tobias George Smollett's novel *The Expedition of Humphrey Clinker* (1771). Moll Flanders's son by her brother is also named Humphrey and there is considerable love between them in Daniel Defoe's *The Fortunes and Misfortunes of Moll Flanders* (1722). Humphrey van Weyden is an at-first-ineffectual aristocrat who builds confidence to overcome the formidable Wolf Larsen in Jack London's *The Sea Wolf* (1904). Humphrey Chimpden Earwicker represents the everyman, together with all his foibles, in James Joyce's *Finnegans Wake* (1939).

Isaac—In 1708, Jonathan Swift invented astrologer Isaac Bickerstaff to put a damper on a blowhard colleague, John Partridge. Though he was fictional, Bickerstaff's status grew to real-life proportions when Richard Steele installed him as the editor, albeit imaginary, of *The Tatler*.

Jack—Jacks are generally good chaps who get in and out of scrapes. Jack Wilton is a Jack before his time, as the name seems more suitable among the Toms and Fannys of a century later; he is the raffish protagonist of Thomas Nashe's best-known work, the picaresque novel *The Unfortunate Traveller, or The Life of Jack Wilton* (1594). Jack represents the extreme Protestants in Jonathan Swift's *A Tale of a Tub* (1704). Captain Jack Absolute is Lydia Languish's splendid and chivalrous suitor in Richard Brinsley Sheridan's *The Rivals* (1775). Nursery-rhyme Jacks include thirsty Jack of "Jack and Jill" and the resourceful, courageous Jack of "Jack and the Beanstalk." Jack Dawkins is Charles Dickens's bright and engaging Artful Dodger in *Oliver Twist*. In Oscar Wilde's *The Importance of Being Earnest* (1895), merry suitor Ernest Moncrieff goes by the name of Jack Worthing. Sheriff Jack Potter rides into town without a gun, signaling the end of the Old West in "The Bride Comes to Yellow Sky" by Stephen Crane (1898). Jack Duluoz is Jack Kerouac's alter ego; he represents restless, disenfranchised youth in beat classics of the 1950s and '60s.

Ithuriel—Ithuriel is another angel under Gabriel's command in *Paradise Lost* (1667) by John Milton. His gifts include instant recognition of falsehoods.

James—James is Moll Flanders's favorite husband, whom she calls "Jemy" in Daniel Defoe's *The Fortunes and Misfortunes of Moll Flanders* (1722). James Bond, Ian Fleming's debonair and invincible 007, first appeared in *Casino Royale* (1963) and just keeps sweeping away women and villains, sweatless every time.

Joseph—The original Joseph, a slave in the Old Testament, spurns the advances of his Egyptian master's wife. In *Joseph Andrews* (1742), Henry Fielding depicts the burly virtuous type, devoted to Fanny Goodwill, who loves him back.

Martin—Martin represents the Lutherans in Jonathan Swift's *A Tale of a Tub* (1704). In Charles Dickens's *The Life and Adventures of Martin Chuzzlewit* (1844), old Martin Senior waits out his rapacious son until Martin Junior's experiences in America turn him into a more grateful heir. Dr. Martin Arrowsmith of Sinclair Lewis's *Arrowsmith* (1925) struggles to pursue pure science and is frustrated by the demands of daily life.

Matthew—Matthew Bramble in Tobias George Smollett's *Expedition of Humphrey Clinker* (1771) is a hypochondriacal eccentric. Spellbinding fundamentalist Matthew Harrison Brady represents William Jennings Bryan, prosecuting the evolutionist schoolteacher in Jerome Lawrence and Robert Lee's theatrical account of the "Monkey Trial," *Inherit the Wind* (1955).

Michael—Michael is the warrior archangel, fitted full out with wings and armor, in John Milton's *Para-*

dise Lost (1667). *Michael Kohlhaas* (1808) by Heinrich von Kleist quests for justice, a noble type rendered rageful. In Thomas Hardy's *The Mayor of Casterbridge* (1886), Michael Henchard is a lonely, domineering recovered alcoholic for most of the book, during which he nearly succeeds in spoiling everyone's life.

Mirabell—He is the witty and worthy object of Millanant's affection in William Congreve's *The Way of the World* (1700).

Paul—Paul in Bernardin de Saint-Pierre's *Paul and Virginia* (1787) is Virginia's soul mate; raised together, the two die within sight of each other in Mauritius. Paul Morel is the central character in *Sons and Lovers* by D. H. Lawrence (1913); his affection for his mother, who helps him rise above his limiting background, wars with his awareness of her crippling love. Paul Pennyfeather is a boys' school teacher who unwittingly becomes embroiled in the white slave trade, a commerce which he eventually abandons to study theology, in Evelyn Waugh's *Decline and Fall* (1928). Paul is the narrator of Erich Maria Remarque's *All Quiet on the Western Front* (1929); as a member of the Lost Generation that survived the First World War, Paul takes a decided stand against romantic views of combat.

Perry—Tobias Smollett's Peregrine "Perry" Pickle is a lovable if licentious practical joker in *Peregrine Pickle* (1751).

Peter—Peter, the most impetuous of Christ's disciples, represents the Roman Catholics in Jonathan

Swift's *A Tale of a Tub* (1704). J. M. Barrie's flying boy *Peter Pan* (1902) wouldn't grow up. And then, of course, there is Beatrix Potter's naughty little *Peter Rabbit* (1900), whose transgressions ruin his day, his evening, and his jacket. Lord Peter Wimsey, created by Dorothy Sayers in her mysteries of the 1920s and '30s, is a blue-blooded sleuth.

Raphael—Raphael is the healer archangel, charitable and good-tempered, in John Milton's *Paradise Lost* (1667). As the hero of Honoré de Balzac's *The Wild Ass's Skin* (1830), Raphael obtains a magic hide that grants him his every wish—but shrinks as each desire becomes reality.

Robinson—Daniel Defoe's errant traveler *Robinson Crusoe* (1720) adeptly improvises an existence on a deserted island while reflecting on where he went wrong, with help from the Bible.

Theodore—This fine-looking and fearless peasant rescues Isabella from Manfred and becomes the ruler of *The Castle of Otranto* (1764) by Horace Walpole.

Tom—The bawdy and determined foundling, Tom Jones is the consummate adventurer in the engrossing *Tom Jones* by Henry Fielding (1749). In the end, he gets the girl and his inheritance. Fielding also wrote a play about another more diminutive Tom, *Tom Thumb*. Tom Pipes in Tobias Smollett's novel *Peregrine Pickle* (1751) is an inveterate whistler. The dignified Uncle Tom in Harriet Beecher Stowe's *Uncle Tom's Cabin* (1852) is flogged to death by odious Simon Legree. Thomas Bailey Aldrich wrote a fictional biography, *The Story of a Bad Boy* (1870); its mischievous subject was a prototype for Tom Sawyer. The hero of Twain's *The Adventures of Tom Sawyer* (1876) is a shrewd, adaptable chap with a conscience. Tom Canty, the pauper of Twain's *Prince and the Pauper* (1881), finds being a prince a sobering experience. F. Scott Fitzgerald's Tom Buchanan epitomizes the wealthy boor in *The Great Gatsby* (1925). Boy inventor *Tom Swift* is the mid-twentieth-century creation of Edward Stratemeyer (writing as Victor Appleton). Determined Okie Tom Joad, from John Steinbeck's *The Grapes of Wrath* (1939), journeys with his family from the Dust Bowl to California.

Uriel—Uriel is the archangel of light, the sun's own messenger, in John Milton's *Paradise Lost* (1667).

Uzziel—An angel of rabbinical lore, Uzziel's name means "strength of God" in John Milton's *Paradise Lost* (1667).

Wilhelm—Johann Wolfgang von Goethe's *Wilhelm Meister* (1795) is an aspiring young writer who learns about the wealth inherent in a more humble worldview. In *Wilhelm Meister's Apprenticeship* (1824), also written by Goethe, Wilhelm is again a young knowledge seeker.

ROMANCE:

Romantic Movement Names (the first half of the nineteenth century)

❧∾

As if worn out by religious controversy, moralizing, and political strife, writers fell back into a period of intense romanticism during the first half of the nineteenth century. Philosophers and poets of the age led the movement. With a theme of "back to nature" at its core, many writers decried the ill effects of the industrial revolution. Heroines besotted themselves with trying to "tie the knot." Heroes dashed off to achieve deeds of derring-do. Right and left people were again left bleeding for love.

Romantic Movement Women's Names

Andromeda—Andromeda is the daughter of Cepheus and Cassiopeia whose ravishing looks got her chained to a rock, thanks to her mother. She is rescued by Perseus, whom she marries, and afterward casts into the celestial heavens beyond. Charles Kingsley wrote the poem "Andromeda" (1858). She reappears as a fuzzy oval galaxy, the seat of Michael Crichton's *Andromeda Strain* (1969).

Annabel—Annabel is a dying beauty in Edgar Allan Poe's poem "Annabel Lee" (1849).

Anne (Ann)—The good and charming Anne Elliot is the heroine in Jane Austen's *Persuasion* (1818). She has passions she cannot abandon. Anne of Austria, the Spanish queen of France, is lovely to behold but miserable in her queenly role in Alexandre Dumas's novel *The Three Musketeers* (1844). A fabulous teller of yarns is Annie, of "Little Orphan Annie" (1885), a poem by James Whitcomb Riley. *Ann Veronica* is H. G. Wells's protoypical feminist (1909). Anne Frank, avid diarist and Nazi victim, remains an inspiring literary figure.

Aspasia—Pericles' highly cultured courtesan, whose house attracted the pundits of the epoque, is featured in Walter Savage Landor's *Pericles and Aspasia* (1836).

Blumine—Writer Thomas Carlyle's "rose goddess" Blumine throws over the feckless Diogenes Teufelsdröckh in *Sartor Resartus* (1833–34).

Catherine—Socialite and snob Lady Catherine de Bourgh is a character in Jane Austen's *Pride and Prejudice* (1813). Catherine Earnshaw of Emily Brontë's *Wuthering Heights* (1847) is Heathcliff's soul mate, free-spirited and selfish in a way that just won't die. Henry James's good heroine Catherine Sloper, who fears that her fiancé is a fortune hunter, manages to prevail over her abusive father in *Washington Square* (1881). Long-tressed, unconventional Red Cross nurse Catherine Barkley is in Ernest Hemingway's war-torn *A Farewell to Arms* (1929).

Christabel—Christabel is the sweet and devout subject of Samuel Taylor Coleridge's poem by the same name (1816) who is victimized by a female vampire.

Consuelo—George Sand's *Consuelo* (1842) is about a Venetian Gypsy whose operatic voice leads her into the highest European circles.

Corinne—Madame Germaine de Staël wrote *Corinne* (1807) about an English-Italian poetess who dies of grief over love. Nevil is her suitor, but she loves Oswald.

Delphine—Madame de Staël's tragic heroine, Delphine poisons herself after her lover Léonce is shot as a traitor in *Delphine* (1802).

Diane—Honoré de Balzac's exceptional but pitiless noblewoman, Diane de Cadignan, has sex with just about everyone in *La Comédie Humaine* (1841) and is the heroine of *Les Secrets de la Princesse de Cadigan* (1839).

Dudu—Don Juan falls in love with Dudu, a head-turner in a Constantinople harem, in Lord Byron's mock epic *Don Juan* (1819–24).

Elizabeth—Elizabeth Bennet is sharp-tongued and sensible in *Pride and Prejudice* (1813) by Jane Austen. Elizabeth-Jane is Susan Henchard's daughter in Thomas Hardy's *The Mayor of Casterbridge* (1886); a proper young woman, she is not Mayor Henchard's real daughter, but she becomes the future mayor's wife. Angela Carter, modern mistress of the gothic, brought back Lizzie Borden, who gave her parents eighty-one whacks, with a new twist, in two stories from *Burning Your Boats* (1996), "Fall River Ax Murders" and "Lizzie's Tiger."

Ellen—Sir Walter Scott was enamored of the name Ellen and used it often. She is once the bride swept away by Lochinvar in his narrative poem *Marmion* (1808), and appears later in his *The Lady of the Lake* (1810), where Malcolm Graeme is a daring suitor to fair Ellen Douglas of Loch Katrine. Unconventional and passionate Ellen Olenska tempts Newland Ancher to abandon his predictable future in Edith Wharton's *The Age of Innocence* (1920).

Emma—In the novel of that name by Jane Austen (1816), Emma Woodhouse is charming and quick-witted. Compelled to make the best of a time when smart women had too little to do, she busies herself in meddling. Gustave Flaubert's Emma is the tirelessly aspiring but mediocre *Madame Bovary* (1856), whose romantic aspirations and profligacy bring ruin to her husband, amputation to the local cripple, insurmountable debt, and death by poison. Emma Clere is the beloved of James Joyce's character Stephen Dedalus in *A Portrait of the Artist as a Young Man* (1916).

Esmeralda—The ravishing Gypsy dancer of this name captures Quasimoto's heart when she seeks refuge in the cathedral, in *The Hunchback of Notre Dame* (1831) by Victor Hugo.

Etarre—Considered an unintellectual version of Vivien, the Lady of the Lake, Etarre is the object of old Pelleas's affections in Alfred, Lord Tennyson's "Pelleas and Etarre," from his *Idylls of the King* (1859–85).

Eugénie—Honoré de Balzac created *Eugénie Grandet* (1833), a young woman whose wretched father ruins her chances of happiness.

Evangeline—Henry Wadsworth Longfellow composed *Evangeline, A Tale of Acadia* (1847) about Evangeline Bellefontaine and Gabriel Lajeunesse, two star-crossed lovers during the British invasion of Nova Scotia. They don't reunite until Gabriel is on his deathbed.

Fanny—Women with this name seem to issue from poor beginnings. Not especially pretty, but proper and unassuming Fanny Price in Jane Austen's *Mansfield Park* (1813) has virtues that are rewarded in the end. In Thomas Hardy's *Far from the Madding Crowd* (1874), the impoverished Fanny Robin dies giving birth to her bastard child. Fanny Price is also a character in W. Somerset Maugham's *Of Human Bondage.* An art student and sensitive type, she commits suicide.

Fayaway—Fayaway is an exotic Polynesian woman who nurses the hero after a leg wound in Herman Melville's *Typee* (1846).

Geraldine—Geraldine is a supernatural specter of evil, seductive on the outside, scaly on the inside, in Samuel Taylor Coleridge's poem "Christabel" (1816).

Godiva—The wife of Leofric, a Saxon earl, thankfully has hair enough to cover her foray in the buff. Naked, she rides her horse through town on a wager, so her husband will reduce taxation. She is the subject of one of Walter Savage Landor's *Imaginary Conversations* (1829) and Tennyson's "Godiva" (1842).

Gretchen—Gretchen the wench is another of Faust's conquests in Johann Wolfgang von Goethe's *Faust* (1808).

Haidée—Haidée is the beautiful Greek daughter of Lambro, with whom Don Juan falls in love in Lord Byron's mock epic *Don Juan* (1819–24).

Ianthe—Ianthe is a poet's fabrication. Lord Byron, Walter Savage Landor, and Percy Bysshe Shelley all addressed poems to this fictional woman.

Indiana—George Sand's Creole heroine, Indiana, is swept away from a staid marriage by a younger lover in *Indiana* (1932), as was Sand herself.

Inez—Inez is Don Juan's prudish mother in Lord Byron's poem *Don Juan* (1819–24).

Ione—In love with Glaucus, Ione is unable to consummate her passion until the eruption of Vesuvius allows them to escape together in Edward Bulwer Lytton's *The Last Days of Pompeii* (1834).

Jane—Jane is the loveliest of the five Bennet sisters in Jane Austen's *Pride and Prejudice* (1813). She is later the forthcoming and able governess *Jane Eyre* (1847) by Charlotte Brontë. Eyre had a miserable childhood, which parents using this name must not inflict. Jane is Tarzan's ideal mate, willing

Lord Byron's life seems every bit as romantic as his work and the literary period he defines. George Gordon, Sixth Baron Byron (1788–1824) was a busy man. He wrote poetry, answered criticism in couplets, and was a member of the House of Lords. Long poems describing his travels in Portugal, Spain, and Greece centered on Childe Harold, the quintessential Byronic hero—a handsome, tempestuous loner, just like Lord Byron himself. Byron's wife of one year, Anne Isabella Milbanke, left him, then rumors of incest with his half sister Augusta drove him out of England. Many people thought he was insane, but never mind, Lord Byron moved to Italy and started a literary journal, which didn't last long. There, he completed Don Juan, a mock epic in sixteen cantos satirizing British life. Hearing of the Greek insurgents' struggle for independence from the Turks, he hustled off to join them. He enlisted a regiment and gave large sums of money to the cause. He died of a fever in Missolonghi, a town in western Greece.

to forgo fripperies to swing through the jungle canopy with him in Edgar Rice Burroughs's *Tarzan of the Apes* (1914) and subsequent Tarzan books. Jane is the first name of the busybody sleuth and knitter, Miss Marple, from twentieth-century detective-story writer Agatha Christie. William Butler Yeats conceived a wildly unconventional Crazy Jane in a series of poems (1933). Jane, a former slave, recounts her hundred years of striving for civil rights in Ernest J. Gaines's *Autobiography of Miss Jane Pittman* (1971).

Judith—In the Old Testament Judith is the brave beheader of Holofernes. In *Judith* (1841), playwright Friedrich Hebbel made Judith Holofernes's lover as a way for her to get close to his head. Jean Giraudoux did the same thing in 1931. William Faulkner's Judith Sutpen is another take-action sort of woman in *Absalom, Absalom!* (1936).

Lamia—Lamia is a phantom woman in serpent form who exudes the illusion of beauty and grace in the poem *Lamia* by John Keats (1820).

Leilah—Lord Byron created this marvelous-looking Turkish concubine who flees with a Christian to her demise in "Leilah" (1813).

Ligeia—Edgar Allan Poe wrote of "Ligeia" (1838), a beloved wife who dies and later comes back to life.

Lucy (Lucie)—Lucy is the sportive and comely inspiration for five "Lucy" poems by William Wordsworth (1799). Cunning, upwardly mobile Lucy

Steele appears in Jane Austen's *Sense and Sensibility* (1811). Lucy Ashton, from Sir Walter Scott's *Bride of Lammermoor* (1819), goes mad with grief for having to marry someone she does not love, stabs the groom, and herself dies the next day in convulsions. Lucy is Richard Feverel's wife, who garners love above her social station, in George Meredith's novel *The Ordeal of Richard Feverel* (1859). Around the good and lovely Lucie Manette turns Charles Dickens's *A Tale of Two Cities* (1859). E. M. Forster, too, had his Lucy, Lucy Honeychurch, who finally succumbs to George Emerson's natural and passionate nature and rejects the tedious Cecil Vyse in *A Room with a View* (1908). In C. S. Lewis's *The Chronicles of Narnia* (1950–56), Lucy Pevesnie is transported to Narnia, learns, and triumphs over and again.

Lucrezia (Lucretia, Lucrèce)—Lucretia is a Roman rape victim who stabs herself. This unhappy plotline is the stuff of at least a half dozen chronicles of the seventeenth through the nineteenth centuries. Depictions of another Lucrezia, a real-life member of the greedy Borgia bunch, impute her with all-around degeneracy—incest, illegitimate children, and deftness with a vial of poison. Probably she was not that bad. She appears in a play by Victor Hugo, *Lucrèce Borgia* (1833), and an opera, *Lucrezia Borgia* (1833), by Gaetano Donizetti.

Lydia—Lydia Languish is the sought-after prize in Richard Brinsley Sheridan's *The Rivals* (1775). She is also the next-to-youngest of the five Bennet sis-

ters in Jane Austen's *Pride and Prejudice* (1813), a
self-absorbed little hussy. Lydia Ivanova is a pre-
tentious socialite in *Anna Karenina* (1876) by Leo
Tolstoy. Lydia Melford is Matthew Bramble's
niece, who has fallen in love with an unsuitable
man, in *The Expedition of Humphrey Clinker* (1771)
by Tobias Smollett. Lydia Lensky, a widowed Polish woman, is in exile in D. H. Lawrence's *The
Rainbow* (1915).

Marianne—Extravagant emotional displays distin-
guish Marianne Dashwood from her sister Elinor in
Jane Austen's *Sense and Sensibility* (1811).

Marie—Marie de Verneuil is a beguiling spy in Honoré de Balzac's *Les Chouans* (1829).

Maud (Maude)—John Greenleaf Whittier composed
a nostalgic poem in pining after an unconsummated
meeting with a rustic beauty, *Maud Muller* (1854).
In his poem "Maud" (1855), which satirizes femi-
nism, Tennyson describes a "queen rose of the rose-
bud garden of girls." Slight, bright, pretty, and
plucky poet Maude Brewster becomes a pivotal
character in Jack London's *The Sea Wolf* (1904).

Medora—Medora is the true love of "The Corsair"
(1814), a poem by Lord Byron.

Meg—Meg Merrilies is a mad, exotic Gypsy in Sir
Walter Scott's *Guy Mannering* (1815), so great and
compelling a character that she inspired a poem
"Old Meg, She Was a Gypsy" of the same time by
John Keats.

Pocahontas—As a Native American word, Pocahontas means "playful." A real-life figure, she became legendary as a symbol of rapprochement between natives and colonials and is often referred to in literature as such. Early on, John Davis featured Pocahontas in his *First Settlers of Virginia* (1805), J. N. Barker in *The Indian Princess* (1808), and J. E. Cooke in *My Lady Pokahontas* (1885).

Rapunzel—In *Grimms' Fairy Tales* (1857), the folktale of Rapunzel found publication. Her golden tresses, longer by triple than Godiva's, allow her lover to climb into the tower where she has been locked away by her guardian.

Rebecca—Rebecca, the daughter of Isaac the Jew, is the real heroine of Sir Walter Scott's *Ivanhoe* (1818), though Wilfred, knight of Ivanhoe, chooses Rowena instead. Another Rebecca is a ubiquitous specter in Daphne du Maurier's book of the same name (1938); her lingering influence twists the lives of each character.

Ulalume—Edgar Allan Poe wrote a poem "Ulalume" (1847) about a true love who has died.

Zémire—Zémire is a myopic "Beauty" in André Getry's late-eighteenth-century rendition of "Beauty and the Beast," *Zémire and Azor*.

Zenobia—Zenobia, once the defiant, powerful, and ambitious queen of Palmyra, east of Syria, takes on a new identity in Nathaniel Hawthorne's *The Blithedale Romance* (1852)—that of a regal,

dark-haired woman of letters whose affections are
spurned.

Romantic Movement Men's Names

Aramis—Aramis is devout, circumspect, and romantic, a brave musketeer in Alexandre Dumas's novel
The Three Musketeers (1844).

Athos—Wise, temperate, and courageous, Athos is the
most mature of *The Three Musketeers* (1844) by
Alexandre Dumas.

Auguste—Amateur snoop C. Auguste Dupin solves
mysteries using deduction in Edgar Allan Poe's
"The Murders in the Rue Morgue" (1841) and "The
Purloined Letter" (1845).

Azor—Azor, a prince turned into a beast, tends a rose
as he aspires to be loved by Zémire, in André Getry's late-eighteenth-century rendition of "Beauty
and the Beast," *Zémire and Azor*.

Beppo—Although he spends the bulk of the poem
abroad in Lord Byron's "Beppo" (1818), Beppo is
somehow considered a fabulously heroic husband to
the rhapsodic Laura, whom he leaves behind.

Brandon—The gracious and honorable Colonel Brandon behaves admirably throughout Jane Austen's
Sense and Sensibility (1811).

Chingachkook—Cunning and wise, Chingachkook is
the last Mohican of James Fenimore Cooper's *The*

Last of the Mohicans (1826), a Delaware chief known as "le Gros Serpent," the big snake.

Conrad—Lord Byron's wily Greek pirate in *The Corsair* (1814), Conrad sneaks in and sneaks out of a sultan's palace at will.

Dandie—The eccentric and entertaining farmer Dandie Dinmont, also a dog lover, is in Sir Walter Scott's *Guy Mannering* (1815).

Daniel—The fictionalized Daniel Boone is a real American remake of the biblical Daniel, who was divinely delivered from a den of lions. James Fenimore Cooper and Lord Byron rhapsodized about this fearless American frontiersman in the nineteenth century. A man of great character, Daniel Deronda turns to Jewish nationalism when he learns of his Jewish roots in the novel *Daniel Deronda* by George Eliot (1876).

D'Artagnan—This bold, irreverent, and highly appealing hero of Alexandre Dumas's historical novel *The Three Musketeers* (1844) has far-reaching goals and chivalrous intent.

David—A good huntsman, since he slew Goliath with a slingshot, David reappears as the both real and legendary frontiersman Davy Crockett, able scout and a terrific marksman, in *A Narrative of the Life of David Crockett* (1834). Charles Dickens's intelligent and sensitive *David Copperfield* (1849–50), a different type, also seeks to be a hero in his own life. Teenage orphan David Balfour eventually over-

comes his villainous uncle, but with exertion suffi-
cient to turn Robert Louis Stevenson's *Kidnapped*
(1886) into a classic. Then, of course, there is Davy
Jones, the sea-fiend host to all drowned sailors, frequently referred to throughout literature.

Dietrich—Torpid but dear Dietrich Knickerbocker
appears in Washington Irving's *A History of New
York from the Beginning of the World to the End of
the Dutch Dynasty* (1809).

Edward—The honorable Edward Ferrars takes a
while to resolve his love life in Jane Austen's *Sense
and Sensibility* (1811). Edward Fairfax Rochester is
Jane's dashing and energetic hero in *Jane Eyre*
(1847) by Charlotte Brontë. He gets the girl, but alas
not until he is blind and has one hand amputated.
And then there is Edward Hyde, Robert Louis Stevenson's furry scuttering Neanderthal, in *Dr. Jekyll
and Mr. Hyde* (1883). Captain Edward Vere, biblio-
philic and aristocratic, sentences Billy to die in Herman Melville's *Billy Budd* (1901).

Eugene (Eugène)—Eugène de Rastignac in Honoré
de Balzac's *Le Père Goriot* (1834) is transformed
over the course of the novel from naive to unre-
strainedly ambitious. The wily guy improves his lot
via the beds of Père Goriot's offspring. Aleksandr
Pushkin wrote *Eugene Onegin* (1831) about a shallow, drama-seeking aristocrat. Eugene Witla, in
Theodore Dreiser's *The Genius* (1915), is an immensely successful art director before his wife's
death reorients him. Young Eugene Gant's sensitiv-

ity and energy propel him into a romantic pilgrimage, a far cry from his claustrophobic small-town upbringing, in Thomas Wolfe's *Look Homeward, Angel* (1929). In John Knowles's *A Separate Peace* (1960), adolescent Gene learns trust and self-dependence the hard way.

Felix—Felix, overbearing father in Honoré de Balzac's *Eugénie Grandet* (1833), ruins his daughter's chances of happiness. Henry James wrote of Felix Young in *The Europeans* (1878), a portrait artist painting his way into New England society. In *Confessions of Felix Krull, Confidence Man* (1954), Thomas Mann presents a charming but irresponsible young man.

Francis—Francis Marion, real man turned legend, is the "Swamp Fox." In several books of that name, Francis organizes a rough band of freedom fighters to support South Carolina in the American Revolutionary War. William Cullen Bryant wrote "The Song of Marion's Men" (1831).

Frank—Written by Captain Frederick Marryat, the nautical trials and glories of *Frank Mildmay* (1829) entirely captivated nineteenth-century boys. Business mogul Frank Algernon Cowperwood's zeal for power fails to bring him peace in Theodore Dreiser's *Financier* trilogy (1912–47).

Gebir—This Spanish prince eventually perishes for love of an Egyptian queen in the poem "Gebir" (1798) by Walter Savage Landor.

Geraint—Brave Arthurian knight, Geraint becomes a bit "spleenful," in "Geraint and Enid," from Alfred, Lord Tennyson's *Idylls of the King* (1859–85). He loves Enid as he loves the light of heaven, usually from astride a horse.

Glaucus—In love with Ione, Glaucus is unable to consummate his passion until the eruption of Vesuvius allows them to escape together in Edward Bulwer Lytton's *The Last Days of Pompeii* (1834).

Heathcliff—This brooding, brutal hero loves his Catherine with a passion that outlasts her life in Emily Brontë's *Wuthering Heights* (1847).

Horatius—Thomas Macaulay wrote of Horatius, a hero of ancient Rome who takes on the entire Etruscan army in *Lays of Ancient Rome* (1842).

Hyperion—The brilliant and golden Titan god of the sun gives up his post to Apollo after the fall of the Titans. He is the subject of John Keats's unfinished *Hyperion* (1820–21).

Ivan—Lord Byron recorded the thrilling adventures of Ivan Mazeppa, a Cossack hit man in *Mazeppa* (1819). Ivan Petrovich Belkin in Aleksandr Pushkin's *Tales of Belkin* (1830) achieves his own sort of fame. Ivan is the tortured intellectual in Dostoyevsky's *The Brothers Karamazov* (1879–80); he exemplifies a man robbed of faith. In *The Death of Ivan Ilyich*, Leo Tolstoy shows what a busy repository is the brain of a dying man. Aleksandr Solzhenitsyn's Ivan is a study in complacency and diligence in *One Day in the Life of Ivan Denisovich* (1962).

Ivanhoe—Wilfred, knight of Ivanhoe, though in love with his father's ward Rowena, is tempted by Rebecca in Sir Walter Scott's *Ivanhoe* (1819).

Jean—Swashbuckling freebooter and smuggler Jean Laffite is the subject of many legends, particularly those concerning the War of 1812, in which he fought honorably under Andrew Jackson. Jean Valjean is the ill-fated and honorable hero of *Les Misérables* (1862) by Victor Hugo, many of the pages of which he devotes to saving other characters. For his troubles, Valjean spends much time zigzagging through Parisian sewers and in prison. Jean Christophe Kraft is a cynical artist at odds with the moral disintegration around him in Romain Rolland's *Jean Christophe* (1913).

Juan—This sociopathic rake first appears in Tirso de Molina's *El Burlador de Sevilla* and so on in compositions by Molière, George Bernard Shaw, Alfred de Musset, Honoré de Balzac, Gustave Flaubert, and Aleksandr Pushkin. The mock epic *Don Juan* (1819–24) by Lord Byron describes a different, more responsible lad who is emboldened to discover his past.

Julian—Politics stymie Julian Peveril's romantic pursuits in Sir Walter Scott's *Peveril of the Peak* (1822). Stendhal's Julien Sorel—naïve, arrogant, ambitious, and romantic—is an early French version of the white liberal in *The Red and the Black* (1833).

Kurt Vonnegut's multimillionaire Julian Castle
turns to philanthropy in *Cat's Cradle* (1963). Edward Bellamy's character Julian West is an insom-
niac—not a good quality in a loved one—who lives
for a century in a suspended state, only to awaken
bewildered in *Looking Backward* (1897).

Kit—Charles Dickens's Kit Nubbles is an awkward
but helpful young boy with a wide mouth in *The
Old Curiosity Shop* (1840). Trapper and scout Kit
Carson's bravery and craftiness are described in
many accounts of the Old West, including Joaquin
Miller's poem "Kit Carson's Ride" (1871) and
Willa Cather's *Death Comes to the Archbishop*
(1927).

Knightley—Mr. Knightley from *Emma* (1816) by
Jane Austen is a frank, wise, and likable friend of
the Woodhouse family. Though he is Emma's only
critic, he chastises her in a way that pulls the characters together in happily-ever-afters by the book's
end.

Kubla—Grandson of the legendary Mongolian Genghis Khan, Kubla has flashing eyes and floating hair
in Samuel Taylor Coleridge's poem "Kubla Khan"
(1816).

Lavengro—Lavengro is a philologist who falls in
with a company of Gypsies in George Borrow's
Lavengro (1851).

Leofric—A Saxon earl married to Godiva (of the hair)
is the subject of one of Walter Savage Landor's
Imaginary Conversations (1829).

Léonce—Beloved of Delphine, Léonce is shot as a traitor in Madame de Staël's tragedy *Delphine* (1802). She based Léonce on her lover of seventeen years, Benjamin Constant, author of the classic of romantic youth, *Adolphe*.

Lochinvar—Lochinvar, "daring in love and dauntless in war," is knight of the highlands in Sir Walter Scott's narrative poem *Marmion* (1808). He gallops into a marriage and during a dance makes off with the bride, fair Ellen, swinging her onto his saddle behind him. He thought the groom was a laggard.

Locksley—Locksley is Robin Hood's assumed name in Sir Walter Scott's *Ivanhoe* (1819). It is also the name of the Nottinghamshire town where Robin Hood was born.

Lycius—Lycius, though otherwise temperate, tragically falls in love with the she-serpent Lamia in John Keats's poem *Lamia* (1819).

Malcolm—In Sir Walter Scott's *Lady of the Lake* (1810), Malcolm Graeme makes a daring suitor to Ellen Douglas of Loch Katrine.

Natty—The incorruptible outdoorsy type Natty Bumppo runs bare-chested through *The Last of the Mohicans* and others of *The Leatherstocking Tales* by James Fenimore Cooper (1826).

Nevil—Madame Germaine de Staël wrote *Corinne* (1807) about an English-Italian poetess who dies of grief over love. Nevil is Corinne's suitor, but she loves Oswald.

Nigel—In *The Fortunes of Nigel* (1822), Sir Walter Scott created Nigel Olifaunt, a gallant and vindictive hero who saves lives on the way to vengeance.

Oswald—Madame Germaine de Staël wrote *Corinne* (1807) about an English-Italian poetess who dies of grief over love. Nevil is her suitor, but she pines for the incomparable Oswald.

Pelleas—Elaine's father in "Pelleas and Etarre," from Alfred, Lord Tennyson's Arthurian *Idylls of the King* (1859–85). Pelleas asks Gawain to plead his cause with Etarre, who rejects him.

Porthos—Vain and slightly thick but fearless, Porthos is a loyal musketeer of Alexandre Dumas's *The Three Musketeers* (1844).

Quentin—Sir Walter Scott's novel *Quentin Durward* (1823) is about a chivalrous young member of the Scottish Guard who rescues Louis XI. William Faulkner's Quentin Compson is a deeply disturbed man with a fixation on his sister. He commits suicide at Harvard in *The Sound and the Fury* (1929). The sister, Caddy, names her daughter Quentin, after her brother. Quentin Compson also figures in the narrative that frames the antebellum drama of Faulkner's *Absalom, Absalom!* (1936).

Rip—Washington Irving's "Rip Van Winkle" (1819) is tired. A man drawn away from his nagging wife to tenpins and brew, Rip sleeps until he can sit on his beard.

Robert (Rob)—Rob is the nickname of Robert Macgregor, a kilted Robin Hood type in Sir Walter

Scott's *Rob Roy* (1817). In Scott's *Kenilworth* (1821), Queen Elizabeth so favors Robert Dudley that she makes him the earl of Leicester and a Knight of the Garter. Dudley subsequently kills his wife. Conceited Robert Ferrars is in Jane Austen's *Sense and Sensibility* (1811). The dashingly attractive but puzzling Robert Lovelace in Samuel Richardson's *Clarissa Harlowe* (1747–48) is of highly questionable honor. Kate Chopin's character Robert Lebrun never consummates his affection for Edna because he cannot see her other than as another man's possession, in *The Awakening* (1899). Robert Cohn shows restraint compared with the rest of the characters in Ernest Hemingway's *The Sun Also Rises* (1926), but he is wildly jealous. Another Hemingway Robert, American operative Robert Jordan, is in *For Whom the Bell Tolls* (1940). An idealistic academic, Jordan falls in love with Maria and carries out his assignment as a guerrilla in the Spanish Civil War. Rebellious soldier Robert E. Lee Prewitt is eventually destroyed by his own inability to conform in James Jones's *From Here to Eternity* (1951).

Sobakevich—Sobakevich, in Nicholai Gogol's *Dead Souls* (1842) is an enormous man with an enormous appetite.

Uncas—This confident, assertive young brave is the next-to-the-last Mohican in James Fenimore Cooper's *The Last of the Mohicans* (1826).

Victor—Victor is the given name of Mary Wollstonecraft Shelley's monster-making doctor in *Franken-*

stein (1818). Not an unsympathetic man, the mad genius type, Victor Frankenstein is also known as the "modern Prometheus."

William—Bright, capable William Price is Fanny's dear brother in Jane Austen's *Mansfield Park* (1813). Captain William Kidd is the notorious Scottish pirate who buries a never-to-be-disinterred treasure in James Fenimore Cooper's *The Water Witch* (1830). Willie Stark, on the other hand, is a fictionalized Huey Long. He rises from farm-boy beginnings to become a pompous, corrupt, and insatiably power-hungry governor in *All the King's Men* (1946) by Robert Penn Warren. Willy Loman, Arthur Miller's exquisitely crafted has-been, is the center of *Death of a Salesman* (1949). Willie Keith, a wealthy New Yorker, overcomes his own over-intellectuality to take command of the *Caine* in Herman Wouk's *The Caine Mutiny* (1951).

THE REALIST IMPERATIVE:
Realistic Movement Names (the second half of the nineteenth century)

❧ ❧

$\mathscr{P}$ARENTS will find that the Victorian Age ushered in a new literature, born of the industrial revolution and rising social concerns. Towns grew into cities and resultant societal ills renewed the impetus for reform. Interest in the scientific principles of the age encouraged naturalism. New colonialism and influences from the East and from the Americas began to create a more global literature. An uneasy relationship between social convention and human desire overtook mid-nineteenth-century characters. Novels depicted ordinary people rather than nobility, and being "queer fish," as Lytton Strachey described them, they held the readers' attention.

Realistic Period, Women's Names

Aglaya—Prince Myshkin's wishful fiancée is in *The Idiot* by Fyodor Dostoyevsky (1868). Aglaya is also the name of one of the mythological three graces.

Alice—Lewis Carroll's heroine is curious, considerate, and a bit of a know-it-all in *Alice in Wonderland* (1865) and *Alice Through the Looking Glass* (1872). Another Alice, in *Alice Adams* (1921), a novel by Booth Tarkington, has outlandish fantasies but winds up learning the practical skills of typing and stenography.

Amy—Amy Dorrit, or *Little Dorrit* (1855–57), is one of Dickens's most admirable characters; she is un-corrupted by life inside and outside the prison where she was raised. Another Amy is the most stylish March sister in Louisa May Alcott's *Little Women* (1868).

Anna—The most remarkable Anna is the bright, beau-tiful *Anna Karenina* (1876) by Leo Tolstoy, who, due to uncontrolled passions, throws it all away, in-cluding herself, under a train. Gertrude Stein's *The Good Anna* (1909) describes a domineering German servant. A different but again passionate Anna finds happier conclusions in Eugene O'Neill's *Anna Christie* (1922). More all-encompassing is Anna Livia Plurabelle, James Joyce's romantic heroine in the inscrutable *Finnegans Wake* (1939); A.L.P., as Joyce called her, represents the universal feminine principle.

Ayesha—In Sir Rider Haggard's *She* (1887), she is a 2,000-year-old queen of a city lost in African caverns. Monstrous and beautiful Ayesha is known as "She Who Must Be Obeyed" (not necessarily a good quality in a baby). The reader wants to stop her before she wreaks any more havoc.

Becky—Becky Sharp is an ambitious young woman who schemes her way out of poverty, undaunted by any obstacle in William Makepeace Thackeray's *Vanity Fair* (1848). Becky Thatcher is Tom Sawyer's spelunking girlfriend in Mark Twain's *The Adventures of Tom Sawyer* (1876).

Beth—Frailest of the March sisters in Louisa May Alcott's *Little Women* (1868), she spends time in a bed jacket and makes readers weep.

Betsy—The unbending and brisk Miss Betsy Trotwood was also exceedingly kind in Charles Dickens's *David Copperfield* (1849).

Cathleen—William Butler Yeats's *The Countess Cathleen* (1891) generously sells her soul to save the starving Irish.

Clara—Clara Peggotty is *David Copperfield*'s reassuring nurse in Charles Dickens's novel (1849). Clara Middleton is a pistol in a pretty package in *The Egoist* by George Meredith (1879).

Cosette—Fantine's frail, abused daughter, whom Jean Valjean rescues in Victor Hugo's *Les Misérables* (1862), matures into a beauty.

Daisy—Henry James's *Daisy Miller* (1878) is pretty but provincial, and her behavior sets her traveling companions on their ears; too late they realize the beauty of her unaffected nature. Daisy Buchanan is a somewhat different story. F. Scott Fitzgerald's creation is the quintessential spoiled WASP—pretty, bored, and irresponsible in *The Great Gatsby* (1925).

Darya—Darya Oblonska, Anna Karenina's sister-in-law, is greatly perturbed by her husband's infidelity, but she remains a dedicated parent in *Anna Karenina* (1876) by Leo Tolstoy.

Dorothea—Idealist Dorothea Brooke's ardent dream of social reform is put off by her marriage to the old and pedantic Mr. Casaubon in George Eliot's *Middlemarch* (1871).

Edith—Edith Leete makes a smart and attractive love interest for Julian West when he finally comes to in Edward Bellamy's *Looking Backward* (1897). This makes sense as she is the granddaughter of the woman he was attracted to when he went to sleep.

Edna—Edna, Kate Chopin's protagonist in *The Awakening* (1899), struggles to know herself within the strict confines of Victorian society, particularly herself as separate from her husband or any other man.

Effi—*Effi Briest* (1898), a novel by Theodor Fontane, concerns a blithe woman who marries the wrong man. She is too at odds with the prevailing social code to remain high-spirited.

Elena—Ivan Turgenev's Elena Stakhova turns down all offers to follow the Bulgarian revolutionary Insarov into the fray in *On the Eve* (1860). Anton Chekhov's beautiful but indifferent Elena Andreyevna is the heroine of *Uncle Vanya* (1899).

Elsie—The Elsie books, by Martha Farquharson, gobbled up by young girls of the nineteenth century, featured the faultless Elsie, whose rather arduous adventures fail to diminish her virtue for twenty-six volumes. *Elsie Venner* (1861) by Oliver Wendell Holmes is another story; her snakelike qualities prevent her from finding a happy life, but her character successfully relates Holmes's belief that the concept of original sin is bunk.

Eliza—Harriet Beecher Stowe's mulatto slave escapes over the Ohio River with her child in *Uncle Tom's Cabin* (1852). Eliza is Tess's sister, whom Tess considers her superior, in *Tess of the D'Urbervilles* (1891) by Thomas Hardy. George Bernard Shaw's bold Cockney Eliza Doolittle transforms from a guttersnipe to a lady in *Pygmalion* (1912).

Estella—Proud, independent Estella Havisham is raised with a cruel but single-minded purpose—to torture men—in Charles Dickens's *Great Expectations* (1860).

Eustacia—The romantic and aspiring Eustacia Vye appears in Thomas Hardy's *Return of the Native* (1878), wherein she causes all sorts of trouble.

Félicité—Félicité abnegates everything except faith in Gustave Flaubert's "A Simple Heart" (1877).

Florence—Charles Dickens's Florence Dombey is a fragile little thing, trying very hard to be better in *Dombey and Son* (1848).

Georgiana—Georgiana is the perfect woman, aside from her birthmark, in Nathaniel Hawthorne's "The Birthmark" (1846).

Gruschenka—Gruschenka is a sexy, playful, big-hearted, and sometimes cunning local woman in Fyodor Dostoyevsky's *Brothers Karamazov* (1879–80).

Gwendolyn—Vain but redeemable Gwendolyn Harleth pines in vain for Daniel Deronda in the novel *Daniel Deronda* by George Eliot (1874–76). Oscar Wilde's Gwendolen Fairfax plays love target to Ernest Moncrieff in *The Importance of Being Earnest* (1895).

Hedda—Henrik Ibsen's well-known *Hedda Gabler* (1890) is a housewife whose ennui sucks the play's characters into a treacherous betrayal and suicide.

Heidi—Heidi is the appealing Swiss miss with an affinity for goatherders in *Heidi* by Johanna Spyri (1927).

Hepzibah—Hepzibah Pyncheon is a proud crone in Nathaniel Hawthorne's *The House of the Seven Gables* (1851).

Hester—Hester Prynne is the free-spirited, proud, and captivating heroine who sloughed off her bloomers while her dislikable husband was overseas, in Nathaniel Hawthorne's *The Scarlet Letter* (1850).

Hetty—Hetty Sorrel, cute and shallow, meets a poor fate when found guilty of murdering her own child in George Eliot's *Adam Bede* (1859).

Iolanthe—Gentle-hearted Iolanthe is an exquisite faerie in W. S. Gilbert's operetta *Iolanthe* (1882). She is banished from faerieland for marrying a mortal and conceiving a "half faerie." Afterward she risks death again for the sake of her son.

Jo—Jo is the most liberated of the March sisters, Louisa May Alcott's alter ego, in her novel *Little Women* (1868).

Lorna—Aristocratic Lorna, abducted by outlaws, is considerate and bighearted even as a child in *Lorna Doone* (1869). She saves John Ridd from her pugnacious clan in the novel by Richard D. Blackmore.

Louisa—Louisa Gradgrind is Josiah's wife who finds untapped self will to leave him in Charles Dickens's *Hard Times* (1845).

Madeline (Madeleine, Madelene)—Madeline Bray is Charles Dickens's frail, lovely, and vaguely sad character, Nicholas's love interest and eventual wife in *Nicholas Nickleby* (1838). Madeline Usher is waning, encoffined, and finally zombified in Edgar Allan Poe's "The Fall of the House of Usher" (1839). Madeline is also the smallest and most unpredictable of twelve little girls in two straight lines in the *Madeline* (1939) books by Ludwig Bemelmans. Exceptionally lovely Madelene gives up hundred-proof whisky to run away with Erasmus the ape in Peter Hoeg's *A Woman and the Ape* (1996).

Maggie—Maggie Tulliver, in George Eliot's *The Mill on the Floss* (1860), has passions that suffocate her good judgment. In *Maggie: A Girl of the Streets* (1896) by Stephen Crane, Maggie, who starts in a state of deprivation and moves downhill from there, finally kills herself. Maggie, the "cat" of Tennessee Williams's *Cat on a Hot Tin Roof* (1955), calls her in-laws' children "nothin' but a bunch o' no-neck monstas" and pretends she's pregnant to help her husband get his inheritance.

Meg—Meg is the oldest and prettiest of the March sisters in Louisa May Alcott's *Little Women* (1868).

Minnehaha—Minnehaha means "laughing water" or waterfall. She is Hiawatha's wife in "Hiawatha" (1855) by Henry Wadsworth Longfellow.

Miriam—In the Old Testament, Miriam roused the Hebrew women to dance. She is a captivating but mysteriously tormented Roman art student in Nathaniel Hawthorne's *Marble Faun* (1860) and a Christian maiden with a Muslim lord in a poem of the same name by John Greenleaf Whittier (1870). In tribute to a woman who much encouraged his early career, D. H. Lawrence wrote poetry to a Miriam and named a sympathetic but finally possessive young woman in *Sons and Lovers* (1913) after her.

Nancy—Charles Dickens's poor, abused Nancy in *Oliver Twist* (1838) gets herself killed by Bill Sikes.

Nancy Manningoe is a William Faulkner character who first appears in a short story called "That Evening Sun." He brought her back in *Requiem for a Nun* (1951); her questionable past ultimately enriches her values and allows her to act in a trustworthy way. Nancy Drew is an invention of Edward L. Stratemeyer (writing as Carolyn Keene); his daughter Harriet Stratemeyer Adams subsequently wrote detective Nancy into and out of more mysteries.

Natasha—Instincts govern both Natasha Rostova's attitudes and behavior in *War and Peace* (1864–69). She reflects the approach to life most favored by author Leo Tolstoy. Natasha is a sexually abused beauty in Fyodor Dostoyevsky's *The Idiot* (1868).

Nora—Henrik Ibsen's engaging Nora, in his play of 1879, *A Doll's House,* is jubilant over her husband Torvald's promotion. This elation dissipates as she tries to come to grips with her lack of freedom in married life.

Olive—The altruistic feminist and lesbian Olive Chancellor appears in *The Bostonians* (1886) by Henry James.

Pearl—Pearl is the strange child of Hester Prynne and Arthur Dimmesdale who comes around nicely in the end in Nathaniel Hawthorne's *The Scarlet Letter* (1850).

Polly—Tom Sawyer's kind aunt Polly waffles between love and discipline in her attempts to raise him in Mark Twain's *The Adventures of Tom Sawyer* (1876).

Priscilla—Sweet Priscilla takes refuge from the horrible Westervelt at the utopian community in Nathaniel Hawthorne's *The Blithedale Romance* (1852). Priscilla Mullins opts for John Alden over Captain Standish in Henry Wadsworth Longfellow's *The Courtship of Miles Standish* (1858).

Proserpine (Persephone)—Proserpine, lovely and unwilling queen of the Underworld, is a favorite topic of Algernon Charles Swinburne's "Hymn to Proserpine" (1866). Margaret Atwood published a book of poems called *Double Persephone* (1962).

Ramona—Helen Hunt Jackson wrote of a willful *Ramona* (1884), half-Scottish, half-Indian, whose passions change national feeling toward Native Americans.

Rhoda—*Rhoda Fleming* (1865) by George Meredith concerns a naive and stubborn but well-intended busybody.

Roxane—Cyrano's cousin is as intelligent as she is pretty in Edmond Rostand's play *Cyrano de Bergerac* (1898). In Mark Twain's *The Tragedy of Pudd'nhead Wilson* (1894), Roxana (Roxy) is a radiant-looking slave.

Salomé—A ravishing Old Testament dancer who demanded John the Baptist's head, Salomé again appeared in Oscar Wilde's *Salomé* (1894) and Hermann Sudermann's *The Fires of St. John* (1897).

Sonya—In Fyodor Dostoyevsky's *Crime and Punishment* (1866), the remarkable Sonya is obliged to become a prostitute to support her alcoholic father.

Sue—Sue Bridehead is an independent and smart character with a distaste for marriage in *Jude the Obscure* (1895) by Thomas Hardy. Susan Henchard's husband sells her, with her baby, for five guineas, something from which she never really recovers in Thomas Hardy's *The Mayor of Casterbridge* (1886).

Tess—Tess is an unfortunate beauty who lives a mess of a life in *Tess of the D'Urbervilles* (1891) by Thomas Hardy. Despite her many fine qualities, she is mistreated by men and dies a pariah of Victorian society.

Verena—Both Olive Chancellor and Basil Ransom vie for the easily influenced and delectable Verena Tarrant in Henry James's *The Bostonians* (1886).

Youman—Lafcadio Hearn wrote the story of a black girl from Martinique who remains loyal to the daughter of her white mistress during a massive slave uprising in *Youman* (1890).

Realistic Period, Men's Names

Alcee—Alcee is a New Orleans womanizer. The protagonist Edna refuses to succumb to his charms in Kate Chopin's *The Awakening* (1899).

Alyosha—Alyosha is as affable and pure as his father is corrupt in Fyodor Dostoyevsky's *The Brothers Karamazov* (1879–80).

Andrey—Fierce, sardonic, and proud Prince Andrey Bolkonsky, in *War and Peace* (1864–69) by Leo Tolstoy, is an impassioned friend and lover.

Arkady—In Fyodor Dostoyevsky's *A Raw Youth* (1875), Arkady, thrown about by tumultuous times, changes his ambitions from wanting riches to wanting to live with dignity.

Basil—Gracious, intransigent Basil Ransom is a Civil War veteran in Henry James's *The Bostonians* (1886). Basil March is a man with moral dilemmas in William Dean Howells's *A Hazard of New Fortunes* (1890).

Bazarov—Bazarov is a nihilistic young intellectual in Ivan Turgenev's *Fathers and Sons* (1862).

Ben—Benjamin's tribe, from the Old Testament, has always been stalwart and brave. Later, Ben Gunn makes a survivor and a kindhearted aid to Jim Hawkins in Robert Louis Stevenson's *Treasure Island* (1883). This proud, intrepid toga-type is good with horses and causes in the novel *Ben Hur* (1880) by Lew Wallace.

Bill (Billy)—Heroic showman and scout Buffalo Bill (William F. Cody) was popularized by E.Z.C. Judson's *The Scouts of the Plains* (1872). Another sharpshooter, Wild Bill Hickok, is eulogized in Captain Jack Crawford's "The Burial of Wild Bill" (1876). Billy Bones is a seafaring old dawg in Robert Louis Stevenson's *Treasure Island* (1883). In

Herman Melville's *Billy Budd* (1901), innocent foretopman Billy, with a speech impediment and well-muscled form, kills his evil tormentor and is hanged. In Kurt Vonnegut's *Slaughterhouse-Five* (1969), Billy Pilgrim plays an optometrist turned time traveler. Don DeLillo's cloistered writer Bill Gray frets that terrorists are shaping the world in *Mao II* (1991).

Bob—Goodly, long-suffering Bob Cratchit is an excellent father in Charles Dickens's *A Christmas Carol* (1843).

Boris—Boris is a guilt-ridden czar in *Boris Godunov* (1825) by Aleksandr Pushkin.

Cedric—In Frances Hodgson Burnett's *Little Lord Fauntleroy* (1886), Cedric Errol is a pampered pantywaist child.

Clifford—Clifford Pyncheon is a namby-pamby old aesthete, devastated by imprisonment, in Nathaniel Hawthorne's *The House of the Seven Gables* (1851).

Clym—Clym Yeobright is the bookish title character in Thomas Hardy's *Return of the Native* (1878).

Conrad—In William Dean Howells's *A Hazard of New Fortunes* (1890), Conrad Dryfoos is a son impeded in his yearning for social justice by his father's unrelenting social climbing.

Cyrus—A natural leader, Captain Cyrus Harding leads his band of indomitable castaways over Jules Verne's *Mysterious Island* (1870).

Damon—Reckless ladies' man Damon Wildeve appears in Thomas Hardy's *Return of the Native* (1878).

Diggory—Diggory Venn is a resolution-oriented reddleman and all-around good guy in Thomas Hardy's *Return of the Native* (1878).

Dmitri—Dmitri is the brash and ardent brother among Fyodor Dostoyevsky's *The Brothers Karamazov* (1879–80).

Donald—Donald Farfraeis is a respectable, hardworking corn trader in Thomas Hardy's *The Mayor of Casterbridge* (1886).

Dorian—The indulgent and breathtakingly handsome subject of Oscar Wilde's novel *The Picture of Dorian Gray* (1891) sinks to ever-more-sinful depths; only his portrait shows the effects of his dissipation.

Edwin (Ned)—Ned Cheerble is Charles Cheerble's stout and good-natured brother in Charles Dickens's *Nicholas Nickleby* (1838). Frustrated architect Edwin Clayhanger, from Arnold Bennett's *Clayhanger* series (1910–18), is in conflict with his father.

Enoch—"Enoch Arden" by Alfred, Lord Tennyson (1864) is a seafaring mate who returns to find his spouse remarried.

Ernest—Ernest Moncrieff, also known as Jack Worthing, is the merry suitor to Gwendolen Fairfax in Oscar Wilde's *The Importance of Being Earnest* (1895).

Felix—George Eliot fashioned *Felix Holt, the Radical* (1866), in which Felix repairs timepieces while inciting the underclasses to self-betterment.

Fletcher—Admirable mutineer Fletcher Christian surmounts the abusive and cruel Captain Bligh in Charles Nordhoff and James Hall's *Mutiny on the Bounty* (1932).

Flint—Flint is both a legendary pirate and a parrot in Robert Louis Stevenson's *Treasure Island* (1883).

François—Medieval rogue poet François Villon is celebrated by Robert Louis Stevenson in the nineteenth century and by others in the twentieth. François is the young hero who carves himself a path

Charles Dickens (1812–70) is the author of some of the most beloved stories of all time and the creator of many of literature's most memorable characters. Who could forget such oddball personages as Scrooge and Fagin and Miss Havisham? Though not all denizens of Dickens's novels make worthy namesakes, each brings a special texture to the plots and other characters. Dickens's gift was perhaps not so much for fashioning eccentric people as for observing and recording exaggerations that others might overlook. His legacy, both comic and tragic, fairly bursts with highly original people and dramatic life. Dickensian names cannot help but recall his marvelous insight into nineteenth-century England— challenging, peculiar, and lovable.

toward adulthood in changing South Africa in Laurens Van der Post's *A Story Like the Wind* (1972).

Frederic—The ambitions of Frédéric Moreau in Gustave Flaubert's *Sentimental Education* (1869) make him pitiable, like Emma Bovary. Courageous American ambulance driver Frederick Henry casts off detachment in his love for Catherine Barkley in Ernest Hemingway's *A Farewell to Arms* (1929).

Fyodor—Fyodor is a clumsy and dissolute character in Fyodor Dostoyevsky's *The Brothers Karamazov* (1879–80).

Gerard—In *The Cloister and the Hearth* (1861) by Charles Reade, Erasmus's father, Gerard, a calligrapher, becomes a monk. He is the victim of thwarted love for Erasmus's mother, Margaret.

Harold—The impecunious and charming Harold Skimpole is a delightful dilettante in Charles Dickens's *Bleak House* (1852).

Hiawatha—Hiawatha, at first a vengeful son, becomes a great leader and proponent of peace with the white people in the poem of the same name by Henry Wadsworth Longfellow (1855).

Insarov—Ivan Turgenev created the fascinating Bulgarian revolutionary Insarov, obsessed with freeing his country from the Turks in *On the Eve* (1860).

Hans—Dutch skater Hans Brinker is a generous and determined young man in the book of the same name by Mary Mapes Dodge (1865).

Holgrave—Holgrave is a loyal and brave daguerreotypist with a gift for mesmerism in Nathaniel Hawthorne's *The House of the Seven Gables* (1851).

Jacob—Jacob Marley is stingy in life but admonitory in death in Charles Dickens's *A Christmas Carol* (1843).

Jaffrey—Jaffrey Pyncheon is a vile and unpardonable bastard in Nathaniel Hawthorne's *The House of the Seven Gables* (1851).

Jerome—Anatole France created the funny, charismatic abbot, Jerome Coignard. His shameless behavior embellishes *At the Sign of the Reine Pedauque* (1893).

Jesse—Jesse James was an immensely popular bank robber of the Old West, eulogized in the ballad "Jesse James" (1870s) by an anonymous author.

Jim—Intrepid and resourceful Jim Hawkins is in Robert Louis Stevenson's *Treasure Island* (1883). Jim is Mark Twain's bighearted runaway slave in *The Adventures of Huckleberry Finn* (1884). Joseph Conrad's *Lord Jim* (1900) concerns an adventure-bound Jim who suffers for one moment of cowardice and spends the rest of his life trying to achieve heroism. His charisma leads him to a position of authority in which he is forced to acknowledge his own shortcomings. O. Henry's Jim, in "The Gift of the Magi" (1906), gives up his biggest treasure for love of his wife. O. Henry's reformed burglar Jimmy Valentine is found out when circumstances reveal his deftness at safecracking in "A Retrieved Reformation" (1909). *Lucky Jim* (1954) by Kingsley Amis describes university instructor Jim Dixon, whose circumstances are anything but lucky.

Josiah—Josiah Bounderby is a course and intimidating character in Charles Dickens's *Hard Times* (1845).

Jude—Like Fannys, Judes just naturally have a hard time. The admirable Jude Fawley appears in the far-from-uplifting saga *Jude the Obscure* (1895) by Thomas Hardy.

Konstantin—The muscular and wealthy Konstantin prefers the country to the city in *Anna Karenina* (1876) by Leo Tolstoy.

Lavengro—Lavengro is a philologist who joins a band of Gypsies in George Borrow's *Lavengro* (1851).

Miles—A supposedly dispassionate observer, Miles Coverdale, ultimately reveals his attraction for the exploited Priscilla in *The Blithedale Romance* (1852) by Nathaniel Hawthorne. Captain Miles Standish woos Priscilla Mullins by proxy in Henry Wadsworth Longfellow's *The Courtship of Miles Standish* (1858).

Mowgli—Smart, charming Mowgli is Rudyard Kipling's natural child, a junior Tarzan, raised by creatures with long teeth in *The Jungle Book* (1894).

Myshkin—Myshkin is a man whose goodness over-whelms his passions but nevertheless creates havoc in Fyodor Dostoyevsky's *The Idiot* (1868).

Phileas—Rash but very resourceful hero Phileas Fogg travels the globe in Jules Verne's *Around the World in Eighty Days* (1873).

Pierre—After his early ambitions subside, Pierre Bezukhov, protagonist in Leo Tolstoy's *War and Peace* (1864–69), eventually finds a peaceful pace, after pages and pages of soul-searching and tumult.

Platon—Wise peasant Platon Karatayev's near-mystic clarity helps Pierre Bezukhov through *War and Peace* (1864–69) by Leo Tolstoy.

Newman—Newman Noggs is an ill-kempt but kind-hearted character in Charles Dickens's *Nicholas Nickleby* (1838).

Nicholas—Charles Dickens's warmhearted *Nicholas Nickleby* (1838) shoulders responsibility for his family. By contrast, in George Eliot's *Middlemarch* (1871), Nicholas Bulstrode is a wealthy, Protestant banker publicly pious but with a seedy past. Arthur Koestler's *Darkness at Noon* (1941) portrays Nicholas Rubashov, a man demoralized by a police state, living in fear of death. John Fowles's Nicholas Urfe is a teacher led into a surrealistic nightmare on a Greek island in *The Magus* (1965). Thomas McGuane's Nicolas Payne is a disastrous suitor, but is not lacking in persistence, in what some call an organized nightmare, *The Bushwhacked Piano* (1971).

Queegueg—A prince from the South Seas, Queegueg is a harpooner on board the *Pequod* in Herman Melville's *Moby-Dick* (1851).

Roger—Dr. Roger Chillingworth, a man who deserves to be cuckolded, in Nathaniel Hawthorne's *The Scarlet Letter* (1850), is chilling indeed as he plots to undermine the lovers and their child.

Rudolf—The dashing and noble Rudolf Rassendyl rises to the challenges in Anthony Hope's *The Prisoner of Zenda* (1894).

Sherlock—Sir Arthur Conan Doyle's brilliant detective Sherlock Holmes appeared in books from 1887 through 1927. Scientist, musician, athlete, and cocaine addict all in one, he is one of literature's most fascinating geniuses.

Silas—In George Eliot's *Silas Marner* (1861), Silas the weaver's primary interests are religious cultism and counting his money until the foundling Eppie lands on his doorstep and stirs him out of his lonely obsessions. He then understands the difference between financial and moral wealth.

Simon—Devilishly delightful Captain Simon Suggs appears in the boisterous *The Adventures of Captain Simon Suggs* (1846) by Johnson Jones Hooper. The malevolent Simon Legree in *Uncle Tom's Cabin* (1852) by Harriet Beecher Stowe beats Uncle Tom to death. Another barbarous Simon, Simon Gerty, betrays the American revolutionary cause, turns renegade, and runs away with the Indians, an act Elinor Wylie finds not altogether unreasonable in her poem "Simon Gerty" (1923).

Stephen—In George Eliot's *The Mill on the Floss* (1860), Stephen Guest is a dashing and inconstant fiancé. Stephen Oblonsky, too, Anna Karenina's brother, is inconstant to his wife, Darya, but goodhearted in *Anna Karenina* (1876) by Leo Tolstoy. Stephen Brice typifies the Yankee in Winston Churchill's novel *The Crisis* (1901). James Joyce's Stephen Dedalus throws over his other loyalties to live freely in his quest for spiritual, artistic, and emotional fulfillment in *A Portrait of the Artist As a Young Man* (1914–15) and *Ulysses* (1922).

Svengali—A Hungarian musician, Svengali is a dark and powerful mesmerist in George du Maurier's *Trilby* (1894) whose influence turns Trilby into a great singer.

Sydney—Regrettable Sydney Carton in Charles Dickens's *A Tale of Two Cities* (1859) is an insolent alcoholic who, in the end, does "a far better thing."

Tertius—Though a decent chap, Tertius Lydgate makes a bad choice in wives. Rosamond Vincy leads his life down the tubes, despite his noble pursuit of a medical profession in George Eliot's *Middlemarch* (1871).

Thomas—Colonel Thomas Newcome is the honorable, down-to-earth patriarch in William Makepeace

Thackeray's *The Newcomes* (1855). Another patriarch, though with a more menacing manner, is the imposing Thomas Sutpen in William Faulkner's *Absalom, Absalom!* (1936).

Tim—Crippled little Tiny Tim Cratchit in Charles Dickens's *A Christmas Carol* (1843) exudes love. Tim Finnegan leaped up, living, at his own wake in James Joyce's *Finnegans Wake* (1939).

Troy—The irresponsible but irresistibly handsome Sergeant Troy is a lingering memory for the heroine in Thomas Hardy's *Far from the Madding Crowd* (1874).

Walter (Walt)—Walter Gay is a compassionate man and generous husband to Florence Dombey in Charles Dickens's *Dombey and Son* (1848). Walt Trowbridge heads an underground movement against fascist oppression in *It Can't Happen Here* (1935) by Sinclair Lewis. Walter Lee, a black man, finds the courage to openly demonstrate his people's right to personal dignity in Lorraine Hansberry's *A Raisin in the Sun* (1959). Henpecked Walter Mitty is actually one of the greatest escape artists ever imagined, even if it is only from himself, in James Thurber's "The Secret Life of Walter Mitty" (1939).

Wilkins—In Charles Dickens's *David Copperfield* (1849–50), Wilkins Micawber is an ever-hopeful, if ever-impecunious schemer.

Willoughby—Self-centered Sir Willoughby Patterne's lofty opinion of himself by far exceeds anyone else's in *The Egoist* by George Meredith (1879).

Rudyard Kipling (1865–1936) is regarded as one of the greatest English short-story writers, and his work exquisitely portrays the complex interweaving of Western and Eastern cultures. An Englishman born in Bombay, India, he was brought up, unhappily, in a foster home in England. Kipling is best known for The Jungle Book *and* Kim. *Readers first enjoyed the capers and tribulations of Rudyard Kipling's famous trio in his magazine stories* Plain Tales from the Hills *(1887) and then in* Soldiers Three *(1888). Their exploits are cushioned in Kipling's deep sensitivity to India's exotic and mystical culture, Britain's insoluble military situation in India, and his depiction of the code of the British soldier.*

Shadow Selves in
Twentieth-Century Literature

※ ❦ ❦

*L*ITERATURE of the last century teems with diversity. Darwin, Freud, and wars robbed us of our naïveté and technology freed us up to worry about it. A deeper understanding and, at once, confusion about "what it's all about" threads through books, poems, and plays. You'll find that the characters of novels from the last hundred years are perhaps more flawed but more recognizably like ourselves than those of previous literary periods, though they haven't stopped carrying our imaginations to new heights or inspiring us to greater achievement.

Twentieth-Century Women's Names

Ada—Ada is Dr. Van Veen's sister, with whom he sleeps, in Vladimir Nabokov's *Ada; or Ardor: A Family Chronicle* (1969).

Albertine—In Marcel Proust's *Remembrance of Things Past* (1913–27), Albertine is the narrator's sweet and lively mistress. She is also a lesbian.

Aleta—In Harold Foster's *Prince Valiant* (1943), Aleta, queen of the Misty Isles, marries Prince Valiant. Though she must occasionally return to her island kingdom to avert crises, she spends most of the time in Camelot and Thule raising four children.

Alexandra—Alexandra is one of Willa Cather's courageous and hearty women, survivors on the plains in *O Pioneers!* (1913).

An-Mei—An-Mei is one of *The Joy Luck Club* (1989) by Amy Tan, a great advocate of faith and of women's independence.

Antonia—Antonia, a Bohemian girl, moves to Nebraska and matures into a patient, hardworking woman in Willa Cather's *My Antonia* (1918).

Ayla—Ayla is a *Homo sapiens* raised by backward Neanderthals in Jean M. Auel's *The Clan of the Cave Bear* (1984) and subsequent Ayla books. Though she suffers various torments while growing up, Ayla becomes attuned to the spirit world engendered by the more primitive people. Eventually she mates with handsome Jondalar and uses her abilities to forge Neolithic milestones, such as taming horses.

Barbara—Rómulo Gallegos's *Doña Bárbara* (1929) embodies the spirit of barbarism. In the book of the same name, Barbara intimidates and destroys men.

Lady Barbara Wellesley is the accomplished and self-possessed woman Captain Horatio Hornblower intends to marry in *Captain Horatio Hornblower* (1937) by C. S. Forester.

Belit—In Robert E. Howard's Conan series beginning with *Red Nails* (1936), Belit is a black pirate captain. She freeboots around with Conan before her untimely death. Conan sorely misses her through many stories. She was almost his equal in strength and their bond was strong.

Berma—Berma is grande dame of the theater in Marcel Proust's *Remembrance of Things Past* (1927), recalling Sarah Bernhardt.

Blanche—Blanche is a has-been belle with a gift for home-breaking in Tennessee Williams's *A Streetcar Named Desire* (1947).

Bonnie—Bonnie Abbzug, with long rich molasses-colored hair and a dancer's body, searches for something good to do in Edward Abbey's *The Monkey Wrench Gang* (1975).

Brett—Tantalizing Lady Brett Ashley, a lost and idle alcoholic beauty, spends Ernest Hemingway's *The Sun Also Rises* (1926) in bed with the rest of the characters.

Carol—In Sinclair Lewis's *Main Street* (1920), Carol Kennicott shows a yearning for culture that cannot be met.

Candace—Impetuous and promiscuous Caddy Compson, after a seduction, is sent away from the family home to marry hastily, twice, in *The Sound and the Fury* (1929) by William Faulkner.

Carrie—Theodore Dreiser's Carrie Meeber in *Sister Carrie* (1900), a naive and destitute country girl, is carried off to New York by a married man. She seeks to make a name for herself on the stage.

Cécile—Cécile is a very territorial adolescent who schemes to prevent her father's remarriage in Françoise Sagan's *Bonjour Tristesse* (1954).

Celie—Celie, too often the brunt of abuse, grows into a strong, proud woman in Alice Walker's *The Color Purple* (1982).

Chrissy—Pretty, blond, and "cool as a cucumber," Chrissy initiates the inquiry at the bridge game in Margaret Atwood's "Rape Fantasies" (1977).

Christine—Stephen King's *Christine* (1983) is independent, astute, unpredictable, and possessed. She is a car.

Clea—Clea is a soft, calm artist—the ultimate romantic destiny of the narrator, Darley, in the volume of Lawrence Durrell's *The Alexandria Quartet* that bears her name (1960).

Constance—True to her name in Arnold Bennett's *The Old Wives' Tale* (1908), Constance could just as aptly have been named Prudence. Unlike her sister, she took the road well traveled. On the other hand is Constance or Connie, the Lady Chatterley in D. H. Lawrence's *Lady Chatterley's Lover* (1928). She eschews the austere and sexually spent atmosphere of her marriage to seek sensual and sexual fulfillment with her gamekeeper.

Della—In "The Gift of the Magi" (1906), O. Henry created Della, a woman who so loved her husband that she sold her hair so that she could buy a watch fob for him—not an everyday sort of wife.

Dolores—Stephen King's *Dolores Claiborne* (1992) murders her husband, who deserves it, and becomes a loyal housekeeper. Dolores Haze is Vladimir Nabokov's precocious *Lolita* (1958), a sexy and exploitative adolescent.

Dominique—Howard Roark's feminine counterpart is Dominique Francon. A woman of uncommon beauty and intelligence, she resents the seaminess of the world in Ayn Rand's *The Fountainhead* (1943).

Dorothy—Chief among Dorothys is the dreaming but determined Dorothy from Kansas in Frank L. Baum's *The Wonderful Wizard of Oz* (1900).

Dita—Dita is a pensive beauty with a laugh like a fast brook, a character from *The Fullest Cup* (1947) by Ula Norgrün. Her name means both "Adam's daughter" and "Are you human?" The first words of the book *Sex* (1992) by pop idol Madonna are "My name is Dita."

Eileen—Another character from James Joyce's *Portrait of the Artist As a Young Man* (1914–15), Eileen Vance is a Protestant child with long, white fingers. Stephen Dedalus's family disapproves of her. Happy-go-lucky goofball Eileen in Ruth McKenney's *My Sister Eileen* (1942) flits around Manhattan under her sister Ruth's often aghast eye.

Esperanza—Esperanza is Sandra Cisneros's blossoming young heroine, aiming for a different house in *The House on Mango Street* (1984).

Eula—Countrified beauty Eula Varner, sort of a twentieth-century Helen of Troy, is coveted by every man in her town but not smart enough to survive, in William Faulkner's *The Hamlet* (1940), part of the Snopes trilogy.

Eveline—A young woman who longs to flee from Dublin to Buenos Aires with her sailor suitor, Frank, but doesn't, in a story in James Joyce's *The Dubliners* (1914).

Francie—Betty Smith's sensitive little Francie Nolan is a connoisseur of dimestore candy and books in *A Tree Grows in Brooklyn* (1943).

Franny—J. D. Salinger's Franny Glass is a bright girl whose disillusionment with the phoniness of her college surroundings leads her to a nervous breakdown in *Franny and Zooey* (1961).

Friday—Robert Heinlein's *Friday* (1988) concerns a spunky heroine on the run, helped out by genetically engineered muscles. A courier, she has a live-free-and-love attitude.

Gabriela—*Gabriela, Clove and Cinnamon* (1962) is Jorge Amado's Brazilian classic about a disheveled young woman of unknown race who, once she is washed up, quickly becomes the most eyecatching cook in town.

Gilberte—Gilberte is Swann's social-climbing daughter in Marcel Proust's *Remembrance of Things Past* (1913–27).

Grüsche—Grüsche, a young servant girl, saves a child. She so loves the child that she refuses to hurt him by pulling him out of a chalk circle that a judge draws around him, in Bertolt Brecht's *Caucasian Chalk Circle* (1944).

Isadora—Erica Jong's heroine Isadora Wing is a highly sexual intellectual in quest of a man who meets her erotic fantasies without compromising her independence in *Fear of Flying* (1973).

Janie—Zora Neale Hurston's Janie Starks in *Their Eyes Were Watching God* (1937) is an independent, self-actualizing woman who finds a way to love that feeds her soul.

Jennie—Theodore Dreiser's *Jennie Gerhardt* (1911), though she is labeled "fallen," does everything within her power to support her daughter.

Jewel—Jim falls in love with Jewel, a young Dutch-Malay woman, in Joseph Conrad's *Lord Jim* (1900).

She is practical in many ways, but with an islander woman's belief in prophetic dreams.

Joy—Hulga Freeman's adopted name is Joy, which she never really lives up to, no thanks to her wooden leg, in Flannery O'Connor's "Good Country People" (1955).

Julip—Jim Harrison's smart, sassy dog lover in the story of the same name (1994).

Kamala—This beautiful courtesan teaches the title character consummate sensuality in Hermann Hesse's *Siddhartha* (1922).

Karen—Baroness Karen Blixen, the author's real name, bravely shoulders a coffee plantation in Kenya in Isak Dinesen's *Out of Africa* (1937). In Don DeLillo's *Mao II* (1991), Karen Janey sees no difference between the here-and-now and the here-and-on-TV.

Kerowyn—Mercedes Lackey wrote *By the Sword* (1991) about a chick in chain mail. Kerowyn, a gorgeous tomboy, learns martial arts and wields a magic sword to avenge her father's death.

Kezia—Katherine Mansfield called her childhood self in New Zealand by this name. Find her as Kezia in several stories including "Prelude" (1918).

Killashandra—Killishandra is a musical student who loses her scholarship in Anne McCaffrey's *Crystal Singer* (1982) and subsequent books. Taking a job as a crystal miner, she goes out on a rocket sledge to search for quartz. Her perfect pitch comes in handy. She is a success but excessive exposure to crystal can lead to addiction.

La—In Edgar Rice Burroughs's *Tarzan and the Jewels of Opar* (1918), La is a princess who dwells in an abandoned Atlantean city. A great beauty, she falls hard for Tarzan, who scorns her because he senses she has mated with gorillas.

Lara—Larissa Fyodoronova Guishar is Yury Zhivago's mistress who, though not as much of a philosopher as he is, responds passionately to his beautiful poetry in Boris Pasternak's *Doctor Zhivago* (1957).

Lena—Gertrude Stein's *The Gentle Lena* (1909) is about a dotty but well-intentioned servant. In Joseph Conrad's *Victory* (1915), Lena is Axel Heyst's underappreciated lover; only her death snaps him to his senses. The daughter of Norwegian immigrants in Nebraska, Lena is pretty and industrious in Willa Cather's *My Antonia* (1918). Lena Grove's peace during pregnancy seems rooted to something larger and deeper than the horrific events in William Faulkner's *Light in August* (1932).

Lessa—In Anne McCaffrey's *Dragonriders of Pern* series, beginning with *Dragonflight* (1968), Lessa is a serf girl hiding from a cruel master until she impresses a dragon hatchling. Then she becomes wife to the weirleader and must make a perilous journey through time to save the planet from falls of a deadly force called "Thread."

Lily—Lily Bart is the unfortunate subject of Edith Wharton's ironically titled *The House of Mirth* (1905) who goes from orphanhood downhill to sleeping pills. The painter Lily Briscoe in Virginia Woolf's *To the Lighthouse* (1927), as an outside observer, is fascinated by dissolution in the Ramsay family. In *Run River* (1963), Joan Didion creates Lily Knight, a character who exemplifies her theory that life is a "history of accidents."

Lindo—Lindo, one of *The Joy Luck Club* (1989) by Amy Tan, tries to hold on to her Chinese roots in America.

Lolly—Sylvia Townsend Warner's heroine *Lolly Willowes* (1926) throws over her humdrum routine to become a witch.

Lorelei—In *Gentlemen Prefer Blondes* (1925), author Anita Loos invented the adorable but none-too-bright gold-digger, Lorelei Lee, later played by Carol Channing on the stage and Marilyn Monroe in the movie.

Magnolia—In Edna Ferber's *Show Boat* (1926), Magnolia is the daughter of a schoolmarm and showboat owner who becomes an actress.

Marjorie—Herman Wouk's *Marjorie Morningstar* (1955) follows a middle-class Jewish girl into the world of show business.

Martha—Saint Martha, patron saint of housewives, is a far cry from Edward Albee's virago in *Who's Afraid of Virginia Woolf?* (1962).

Mary—Among literatures many Marys are P. L. Travers's the "practically perfect in every way" *Mary Poppins* (1934) and Mary Lennox, a girl revitalized by the breeze off the moors in Frances Hodgson Burnett's *The Secret Garden* (1911).

Melanctha—Melanctha, though uneducated and underprivileged, is nevertheless highly attuned in Gertrude Stein's "Melanctha" (1909), one of the *Three Lives*.

Melanie—Gentle, kindly, and frail Melanie Hamilton sees only the good in life in Margaret Mitchell's *Gone With the Wind* (1937).

Melissa—Melissa is a melancholy nightclub dancer without a compass in Lawrence Durrell's *The Alexandria Quartet* (1957–60).

Mona—In Kurt Vonnegut's *Cat's Cradle* (1963), Mona Aamons Monzano was an exotic, raised to become a national sex symbol and wife of the Bokonon president.

Nadja—Nadja has a powerful sixth sense in André Breton's *Nadja* (1928). Her intuitions propel her lover through occurrences both commonplace and weird.

Odette—Odette de Crécy is mistress and then wife of Charles Swann, in Marcel Proust's *Remembrance of Things Past* (1913–27). She goes on to other lovers.

O-Lan—O-Lan is Chinese farmer Wang Lung's tireless wife in *The Good Earth* (1931) by Pearl S. Buck.

Oriane—In Marcel Proust's *Rememberance of Things Past* (1913–27), Oriane de Guermantes is an influential Parisian hostess.

Pollyanna—Irrepressibly glad, young Pollyanna sows optimism even among the most negative characters in the novel of the same name by Eleanor H. Porter (1913).

Rachel—Though Rachel wept while waiting for Jacob and then died in childbirth in the Old Testament, Marcel Proust's Rachel in *Remembrance of Things Past* (1927) is somewhat different. She is a prostitute, the mistress of a powerful man, and a great actress. Rachel Verinder is the troubled heiress missing a diamond, in Wilkie Collins's *The Moonstone* (1868), the original English mystery.

Rima—Rima is the natural jungle wench in William Henry Hudson's *Green Mansions* (1904).

Rosa—Nadine Gordimer's white South African Rosa Burger grows up in an anti-apartheid household in *The Burger's Daughter* (1979). Introspective, she reflects much on the political climate and its impact on herself and those around her. Rosa spends the book trying to defect from her upbringing.

Rose—Rose of Sharon, Tom Joad's impractical sister in John Steinbeck's *The Grapes of Wrath* (1939), becomes less so. She offers her breast milk to a starving person after her baby is stillborn.

Sabina—An artist of unfettered and erotic spirit in Milan Kundera's *The Unbearable Lightness of Being* (1984).

Sadie—W. Somerset Maugham wrote of a blithe and promiscuous Sadie, in "Miss Thompson" (1921), whose ebullient ways ultimately seem much more worthwhile than the Christian values imposed on her.

Sarah—In John Fowles's *The French Lieutenant's Woman* (1969), enigmatic and woeful Sarah Woodruff, though dumped by a military man, is still intoxicating. Damon Runyon's quiet and respectable Sarah Brown is a missionary surrounded by gamblers and gangsters in New York City in the twenties in *Guys and Dolls* (1931). In Paul Scott's *The Raj Quartet* (1966–75), televised as *The Jewel in the Crown,* the fascinating Sarah Layton is the central character.

Scarlett—Manipulative, willful Scarlett O'Hara is the cog around which all events turn in Margaret Mitchell's *Gone With the Wind* (1937).

Scout—Jean Louise "Scout" Finch is Atticus Finch's plucky tomboy daughter whose sense of justice and courage are as strong as his in Harper Lee's *To Kill a Mockingbird* (1957).

Selina—Selina Peake Dejong is a Chicago gambler's daughter, a widow and mother who strains against immense odds in Edna Ferber's *So Big* (1924). Barbadian immigrant Selina Boyce appears in Paule Marshall's *Brown Girl, Brownstones* (1959). She defeats racist setbacks through the art of dance.

Sethe—In Toni Morrison's *Beloved* (1987), proud Sethe kills her daughter rather than subject her to a life of slavery.

Sissy—Sissy Hankshaw is Tom Robbins's sexy big-thumbed hitchhiker in *Even Cowgirls Get the Blues* (1990).

Smilla—Smilla Jaspersen, half-Danish, half-Greenlander, knows how to "read ice" and insist on justice no matter the weather in Peter Hoeg's *Smilla's Sense of Snow* (1993).

Sophia—Sophia is the headstrong, adventurous sister in Arnold Bennett's *The Old Wives' Tale* (1908), in contrast to conservative Constance. In William Styron's *Sophie's Choice* (1979), a tenderhearted Polish immigrant attempts to justify her life after the ravages of World War II. She is both haunting and haunted, kept in chaos by her manic-depressive lover Nathan.

Suyuan—The initiator of *The Joy Luck Club* (1989) by Amy Tan, Suyuan works to maintain the mother-daughter bond in cross-cultural San Francisco.

Sula—Toni Morrison's complex heroine is Nel's true friend in *Sula* (1973). She moves from her poor beginnings to maturity in America's cities but when she returns to her hometown, she feels alienated from the one person who had given her childhood meaning.

Suzy—Suzy is a bouncy and resourceful little drifter who aspires to true love in John Steinbeck's *Sweet Thursday* (1954), set on the fringes of Monterey.

Teela—Teela appears in Larry Nivens's *Ring World* (1970), as a member of the expedition to the Ringworld. Teela Brown's luck determines the fate of galaxies.

Teresa (Theresa, Thérèse)—Teresa Sanger, in *The Constant Nymph* by Margaret Kennedy (1924), is confronted by the adult challenges that love brings very early in her life. *Thérèse Desqueyroux* (1927) by François Mauriac is the story of a wife who, finding her marriage a bit thick, attempts to poison her way out of it—sort of a template for the von Bülow incident.

Thea—Willa Cather wrote *The Song of the Lark* (1915) about Thea, a Colorado girl who becomes an opera star.

Tristessa—Tristessa is an aptly named and masochistic young prostitute, broken by squalid conditions in Mexico in Jack Kerouac's *Tristessa* (1956).

Ursula—The character Ursula Brangwen speaks for D. H. Lawrence's own fiery, rebellious nature. In *The Rainbow* (1915), she shows bisexual tendencies and in the sequel, *Women in Love* (1920), she becomes even more liberal and philosophical. Her marriage to Rupert Birkin represents Lawrence's ideal one—passion plus independence. Ursula Iguarán is the matriarch of Gabriel García Márquez's Buendía family in *One Hundred Years of Solitude* (1967) who lives past her 100th year.

Velvet—*National Velvet* by Enid Bagnold is about a determined girl who loves horses (1935).

Ying-ying—Tragedy led to passivity in Ying-ying, one of *The Joy Luck Club* (1989) by Amy Tan, which in turn distorted her daughter's upbringing.

The work of Irish poet and novelist James Joyce (1882–1941) elucidates the psyche's stranglehold on any endeavor. His use of history and mythology, in a sense, created the modern novel. Joyce was born and educated in Ireland. He departed his homeland with Nora Barnacle in 1904; they and their two children lived in Italy and Paris, where he eventually became nearly blind. When the Nazis invaded France, they moved to Zurich, Switzerland. Joyce painted his characters with a stream-of-consciousness technique, dreams, and different voices and styles. He depicted the labyrinthine complexity of realistic situations. His masterpieces, A Portrait of the Artist As a Young Man, Ulysses, *and* Finnegans Wake, *still seem brave and experimental nearly a century later. Joyce's contribution is, in a sense, a travelogue, an intrepid exploration of the large and hitherto impregnable regions of inner minds.*

Zuleika—This mesmerizing beauty visits an Oxford boating contest in *Zuleika Dobson* by Max Beerbohm (1911). As a result, all but one of the undergraduates drown themselves for love of her. The original Zuleika in the Old Testament causes a lot of trouble for Joseph the slave; after he spurns her affections, she has him thrown into prison.

Twentieth-Century Men's Names

Adrian—Named after the famous Roman emperor, Adrian Leverkuhn is a talented composer in Thomas Mann's *Doktor Faustus* (1947). His actions lead to his destruction, but his music is immortalized.

Alan (Alun)—Alun Weaver is an old Welsh poet and rake who moves, with his trophy wife, into a retirement community, in Kingsley Amis's *The Old Devils* (1986). In Michael Crichton's *Jurassic Park* (1990), Dr. Alan Grant is the foremost authority on dinosaurs. Paleontologist turns child-saver in this gripping trip.

Albert—Margaret Kennedy created a most engaging musician, Albert Sanger, in *The Constant Nymph* (1924).

Aleister—W. Somerset Maugham's novel *The Magician* (1909) is based on the life of Aleister Crowley, a quirky and somewhat sinister practitioner of black magic. Crowley was himself a writer.

Alfred—J. Alfred Prufrock is an isolated, obsessive fantasizer in T. S. Eliot's poem of 1911, "The Lovesong of J. Alfred Prufrock."

Alvin—In an alternative colonial history milieu, Alvin Maker is the seventh son of a seventh son in Orson Scott Card's *Seventh Son* (1987) and *Red Prophet* (1988). Blessed with the power of being a "Maker," in these sci-fi creations he battles through his life with the hydrophiliac Unmaker.

Androcles—This lion-taming Roman slave inspired George Bernard Shaw's *Androcles and the Lion* (1912).

Anse—Dutiful old farmer Anse Bundren honors his dead wife Addie's wish to be buried with her family in William Faulkner's *As I Lay Dying* (1930).

Artemio—Carlos Fuentes's character is a Mexican political strongman who abandons his earlier revolutionary convictions for the sake of power. While dying, Artemio weighs his inner conflicts in *The Death of Artemio Cruz* (1962).

Ashley—Scarlett pursues the ineffectual namby-pamby patrician Ashley Wilkes in Margaret Mitchell's *Gone With the Wind* (1937) and we all wonder why.

Atticus—Atticus Finch is the distinguished, brave lawyer who stands up against other whites in his community to defend a black man unjustly accused of rape in Harper Lee's *To Kill a Mockingbird* (1957).

Augie—Saul Bellow's Augie refuses to settle down and eschews stability in favor of spontaneity in *The Adventures of Augie March* (1953).

Bergotte—According to the narrator in Marcel Proust's *Remembrance of Things Past* (1927), Bergotte is a renowned author with a gift for exquisitely crafted expression.

Bernard—Bernard Rieux in Albert Camus's *The Plague* (1947) works toward saving lives in impossible conditions, embodying self-responsibility and commitment.

Bilbo—This heroic hobbit matures to mentor status in J.R.R. Tolkien's *The Lord of the Rings* series (1937).

Camber—In Katherine Kurtz's *Camber of Culdi* (1985), Camber is a venerable character rich in the magic of his kind. As a Deryni, he has advanced mental powers such as telepathy. These sometimes put him at odds with less gifted neighbors who persecute and want to kill him.

Carson—Carson Napier is the resourceful and well-muscled hero of Edgar Rice Burroughs's Venus series, *Pirates of Venus* (1934).

Cash—Cash is the woodworker child in William Faulkner's *As I Lay Dying* (1930).

Charles—Charles Strictland, W. Somerset's Maugham's fictional version of Gauguin, flees the ennui of the "everyworld" for the idylls of Tahiti, where, by the way, he dies of leprosy in *The Moon and Sixpence* (1919). Shrewd and philosophical Chinese sleuth Charlie Chan is featured in Earl Derr Biggers's books of the 1920s and '30s. In John Fowles's *The French Lieutenant's Woman* (1966), wealthy amateur paleontologist Charles Smithson is stopped in his tracks, captivated by Sarah Woodruff.

Christopher—All immediately remember A. A. Milne's concerned and protective Christopher Robin in the Pooh books (1926–28). In *Parade's End* (1950), Ford Madox Ford's character Christopher Tietjens is a member of the English gentry who abandons tradition to follow his heart following World War I.

Chuck—A fair and spunky character, Chuck Mallison, appears in *Intruder in the Dust* (1948) and other William Faulkner stories.

Clyde—In *An American Tragedy* (1925), Theodore Dreiser's Clyde Griffith is an aspiring simpleton, lured by the promise of affluence into committing a crime.

Daneel—Daneel plays robot partner to Elijah Bailey in Isaac Asimov's *Caves of Steel* (1954). He is a steady and true artificial person who sometimes seems all too human.

Danny—Danny O'Neill is author James T. Farrell's alter ego in several of his novels from 1936 through 1953. Astute, Danny, who has an Irish background, rebels against the debauched life of Farrell's earlier creation, Studs Lonigan.

Darl—Highly aware and articulate, Darl is deemed mad by his far-less-insightful siblings in William Faulkner's *As I Lay Dying* (1930).

Dean—Jack Kerouac bestows his freewheeling, jazz-loving character Dean Moriarty with the personality of his good friend Neal Cassady in the beat classic *On the Road* (1957).

Dennis (Denys)—Isak Dinesen's independent Denys Fitch-Hatton, a hunter and guide in Kenya, knows nature to a heart-stopping degree in her *Out of Africa* (1937). Though he loves Baroness Blixen well enough, he also curries favor with pilot Beryl Markham, airborne and otherwise.

Dicken—Sort of a junior natural man, Dicken has a gift for restoring life to the wounded and near dead in Frances Hodgson Burnett's *The Secret Garden* (1911).

Doc—"Doc" is John Steinbeck's name for Ed Ricketts, a wonderfully wise marine biologist who is generous with locals but territorial about his samples in *Cannery Row* (1945). Doc Savage, with his brilliant mind and sculpted body, was a feature in Kenneth Robeson pulps of the thirties and a series of rereleases in the sixties, for instance, *The Man of Bronze* (1965). Doc Sarvis is a born leader, but with few minions in Edward Abbey's *Monkey Wrench Gang* (1975); "bald-domed with a savage visage," Doc has a favorite pastime—neighborhood beautification, usually of the destructive variety.

Doremus—New England editor Doremus Jessup fights against fascist oppression in *It Can't Happen Here* (1935) by Sinclair Lewis.

DuQuesne (prounounced *Dukayne*)—In E. E. "Doc" Smith's *The Skylark of Space* (1928), DuQuesne plays the villain, always kidnapping the heroine and jetting her off to other galaxies.

Elmer—*Elmer Gantry* (1927) is Sinclair Lewis's story of a prototypical self-promoting evangelist.

Emil—In Hermann Hesse's *Demian* (1919), Emil Sinclair is an adolescent confounded; later he realizes ambiguity is the nature of all things.

Ethan—Edith Wharton wrote *Ethan Frome* (1911) about a struggling farmer whose attempt to flee with his lover ends disastrously. They crash into a tree and end up as cripples.

Frodo—Frodo is an exceptionally good hobbit in J.R.R. Tolkien's *Lord of the Rings* series (1937). He enjoys music and simple pleasures but is not without a higher purpose.

Gandalf—*The Hobbit*'s equivalent of Merlin, Gandalf is a wizard who appears when needed in J.R.R. Tolkien's *The Lord of the Rings* series (1937).

Garp—Garp is a natural storyteller, inspired by one mad event after another in John Irving's *The World According to Garp* (1978).

Gavin—Gavin Stevens is unrequited in love, but successful in law in William Faulkner's *The Hamlet* (1940) and other books.

Gregor—Gregor Melekhov, in Mikhail Sholokhov's *And Quiet Flows the Don* (1934) and other novels, vacillates in his allegiances within revolutionary Russia, finding merits in both the communist and White Russian points of view. Franz Kafka's Gregor Samsa wakes up one morning to find himself with a carapace in *The Metamorphosis* (1937).

Gulley—Joyce Cary created Gulley Jimson, a fine, funny, and raucous old artist in *The Horse's Mouth* (1944) and two other novels.

Gus—Gus McCrae is an immensely appealing retired Texas Ranger-turned-horse-rustler-turned-philosopher in Larry McMurtry's *Lonesome Dove* (1985).

Gustav—Thomas Mann created Gustav von Aschenbach for *Death in Venice* (1912). Gustav is a renowned writer and rumored pedophile.

Harry—Alienated artist Harry Haller in Hermann Hesse's *Steppenwolf* (1927) is at odds with technology and hyperaware of the dissolution around him. In Ernest Hemingway's *To Have and Have Not* (1937), Harry Morgan is a resourceful but ill-fated smuggler. Finally, there is the magnetic *Harry Potter* (1999), J. K. Rowling's boy wizard, in the Harry Potter series.

Holden—J. D. Salinger's smart, sensitive, and precocious adolescent Holden Caulfield is *The Catcher in the Rye* (1951). Damaged innocence leads to his intense cynicism about the adult world.

Homer—The original Homer Simpson has his eyes opened to Hollywood's less glamorous aspects in Nathanael West's *The Day of the Locust* (1939).

Howard—Ayn Rand's human god, architect Howard Roark is a man of uncompromising integrity. So are his designs, in *The Fountainhead* (1943).

Huey—Louisiana demagogue Huey Long is the subject of Hamilton Basso's *Sun in Capricorn* (1942) and John Dos Passos' *Number One* (1943).

Humboldt—Humboldt is Saul Bellow's "poet, thinker and problem drinker" in *Humboldt's Gift* (1975).

Jacob—Perhaps inspired by this biblical patriarch, Virginia Woolf wrote of sensitive Jacob Flanders, meant to represent her brother Thoby. His full life echoed after his death in her book *Jacob's Room* (1922).

Jake—Jake Barnes is narrator of Ernest Hemingway's *The Sun Also Rises* (1926). Castrated by a war wound, he is insightful and devoted to Lady Brett. Jake Donaghue's carefree life represents an existentialist worldview in Iris Murdoch's *Under the Net* (1954).

Jay—Ambitious, rich Jay Gatsby is also desperately romantic in F. Scott Fitzgerald's *The Great Gatsby* (1925).

Jeeves—Jeeves is P. G. Wodehouse's marvelously efficient and heroic butler in his books from 1923 to 1957.

Jo—West Coast oil tycoon Jo Stoyte obsesses about aging and dying in Aldous Huxley's *After Many a Summer Dies the Swan* (1939).

Jody—In Marjorie Rawlings's weeper *The Yearling* (1938), Jody is a sweet child forced to mature by what have always seemed unreasonable parents.

Kim—Kimball O'Hara is a young man with a deep appreciation for India's mysticism in *Kim* (1901) by Rudyard Kipling.

Korak—In Edgar Rice Burroughs's *The Son of Tarzan* (1963), Tarzan and Jane have a son. His name is not "Boy." It is Korak. Korak the killer. He's only in the one book and grows up much as his father did, swinging from vine to vine.

Lennie—Lennie Small, who is not small, is a lumbering loving half-wit of prodigious strength in John Steinbeck's *Of Mice and Men* (1937).

Leo—Leo Naphta brings mysticism and antireason to the sanitarium in Thomas Mann's *The Magic Mountain* (1924).

Lev—Aleksandr Solzhenitsyn created Lev Rubin, the devoted communist in *The First Circle* (1968).

Lew—Detective Lew Archer solves crimes without strong-arm tactics in Ross Macdonald's mysteries of the 1970s.

Leopold—Leopold Bloom is James Joyce's exiled *Ulysses* (1922), a charitable but self-conscious antihero whose only gratification is in reverie, not in human interaction. Leopold's being reinforces the personal exile, one of Joyce's central themes.

Lorenzo—Lorenzo is the name given to author D. H. Lawrence by adoring women.

Lucas—Lucas Beauchamps is the proud nonconformist black man in William Faulkner's *Intruder in the Dust* (1948).

Ludovico—In Thomas Mann's *The Magic Mountain* (1924), Ludovico Settembrini cautions against the sybaritic influences of other sanitarium patients. He is the voice of reason.

Manolín—Manolín is Santiago's devoted young apprentice in Ernest Hemingway's *The Old Man and the Sea* (1952).

Marlow—Marlow is the empathetic, philosophical, and hardworking narrator in Joseph Conrad's *Lord Jim* (1900) and again in *Heart of Darkness* (1902).

Meursault—Meursault from Albert Camus's *The Stranger* (1942) is the original existentialist. He refuses to follow conventional prescriptions and feigns neither love nor faith, but finally affirms, on the scaffold, the merit in rebellion. His early words, *Maman est morte hier,* ("My mother died yesterday") do not bode well for the namer, however.

Mitka—Mitka Vekshin, a disaffected Russian revolutionary, becomes a thief in *The Thief* by Leonid Leonov (1927).

Moto—Moto is a sharp Japanese snoop fleshed out by John P. Marquand in detective stories from the 1930s through the '50s.

Mundinho—In Jorge Amado's Brazilian classic *Gabriela, Clove and Cinnamon* (1962), Mundinho Falcão is a highly successful sociopolitical reformer.

Nero—Nero Wolfe is a pudgy couch potato detective in Rex Stout's mysteries (1934–75); his fearless sidekick Archie Goodwin does his bidding.

Nessim—Justine's husband, in name mostly, Nessim is a revolutionary in Lawrence Durrell's *The Alexandria Quartet* (1957–60).

Newland—Attractive Newland Archer's passions are subjugated by social convention in Edith Wharton's *The Age of Innocence* (1920).

Nick—Ernest Hemingway's gung-ho alter ego Nick Adams appears in *In Our Time* (1924) and *The Nick Adams Stories* (1972). Nick Charles, Dashiell Hammett's detective in *The Thin Man* (1932), is refined and charming, just as is William Powell in Thin Man movies.

Oliver—*Oliver Twist* is Charles Dickens's charming protagonist, nameless and divested of his inheritance from birth. D. H. Lawrence's noble savage is the gamekeeper Oliver Mellors in *Lady Chatterley's Lover* (1928). Though intelligent, he remains uncontaminated by society's meaningless trappings... and gets the girl.

Per—Ole E. Rölvaag's *Giants in the Earth* (1924) tells the story of hardworking Norwegian farmer Per Hansa.

Percy—Sir Percy Blakenly is the hero's public persona in Baroness Orczy's *The Scarlet Pimpernel* (1905). He aids aristocrats under siege during the French Revolution.

Perry—Pushing Raymond Burr aside, find Perry Mason, the exceptionally adept advocate created by Earl Stanley Gardner, first in *The Case of the Velvet Claws* (1933).

Piet—Nicolas Freeling wrote of Inspector Piet Van der Valk in *Love in Amsterdam* (1961). The inspector is an unconventional leftist intellectual with an affinity for young people in trouble. He poses as others to get the facts of the case.

Ramón—D. H. Lawrence's Don Ramón is a character in *The Plumed Serpent* (1926). The heroine spots him at a bullfight, the cruelty of which seems to represent his cause—a resurgence of the Aztec religion. Powerfully sexual, Ramón symbolizes the sort of charismatic male intellectual that lures society toward male domination.

Rhett—Strong, handsome, and sardonic, renegade Rhett Butler swoops in on Scarlett again and again in Margaret Mitchell's *Gone With the Wind* (1937).

Rivière—In Antoine de Saint-Exupéry's *Night Flight* (1931) Rivière is an airline boss whose leadership inspires his pilots to a greater sense of responsibility.

Rupert—In *Women in Love* (1920), Rupert Birkin airs D. H. Lawrence's observation that we have allowed intellect and competition to subvert our sensual nature.

Sal—Jack Kerouac, writer and mind-bender, incorporated his own attributes into Sal Paradise in *On the Road* (1957).

Sam—Sam Spade is Dashiell Hammett's rough-and-ready private eye, introduced in *The Maltese Falcon* (1930). Sammy is a self-actualizing young man who works his way into Hollywood in Budd Schulberg's *What Makes Sammy Run?* (1941). Sam Hill is a mythical American chimney sweep.

Santiago—Santiago is the at-once humble and proud Cuban fisherman from Ernest Hemingway's *The Old Man and the Sea* (1952).

Seldom—Seldom Seen Smith is as rare as his name, a professional river rafter and eco-terrorist in Edward Abbey's *The Monkey Wrench Gang* (1975).

Siddhartha—Siddhartha is a handsome, clever Brahman, whom Hermann Hesse depicts as Buddha in *Siddhartha* (1922). Siddhartha transforms from ascetic to businessman to ferryman.

Sky—Sky Masterson is Damon Runyon's seductive high-rolling gambler in *Guys and Dolls* (1931), set in the Big Apple in the twenties.

Sweeney—Sweeney is the brutal sensual capitalist in several of T. S. Eliot's poems.

Tanar—Edgar Rice Burroughs's *Tanar of Pellucidar* (1929) is a hunter in a primitive society living in a separate submagma world at Earth's core.

Tarzan—Edgar Rice Burroughs's fabulous jungle he-man combines the best of all species as he warbles, chest-beating, through *Tarzan of the Apes* (1914) and subsequent Tarzan books.

Thomas—Thomas Sutpen, poor white southerner, aspires to greater things than the fate that meets him in William Faulkner's *Absalom, Absalom!* (1936).

Tomas—Tomas Gomez is an early Martian settler with a wide smile and poetic disposition in Ray Bradbury's *The Martian Chronicles* (1950). Tomas is a skirt-chasing surgeon in Milan Kundera's *The Unbearable Lightness of Being* (1984).

Todd—John Barth's hero in *The Floating Opera* (1994), Todd Andrews ultimately decides suicide is as meaningless as everything else, so why do it?

Travis—John D. Macdonald spun intrigue after intrigue with Florida private investigator Travis McGee in detective stories from 1964 to 1985.

Tyrone—Thomas Pynchon's Lieutenant Tyrone Slothrop inhabits *Gravity's Rainbow* (1973). A childhood victim of Pavlovian conditioning, Tyrone experiences an odd but not uncoincidental synchrony between his erections and bombings. ABM negotiators should have factored him in.

Victor—In John Hersey's *A Bell for Adano* (1944), the self-abnegating Major Victor Joppolo who, with sincerity and determination, labors to restore dignity to the town of Adano.

Wang—Chinese farmer Wang Lung persists despite many hardships in *The Good Earth* by Pearl S. Buck (1931).

Weedon—Mining engineer Weedon Scott rescues White Fang in the 1905 novel of the same name by Jack London.

Wilder—In Ray Bradbury's *The Martian Chronicles* (1950), Captain Wilder sees the pitfalls of human occupation on Mars and is therefore remanded to a stint at Jupiter and Pluto.

Winston—Winston is the introspective, weak-willed antihero in George Orwell's *1984* (1944).

Wolf—A seductively fine physical and mental specimen, Wolf Larsen is also pitiless and runs his vessel with a terrible anger in Jack London's *The Sea Wolf* (1904).

Woodrow—Taciturn and tough, veteran Texas Ranger Woodrow Call appears in Larry McMurtry's *Lonesome Dove* (1985).

Yakov—In Bernard Malamud's *The Fixer* (1966), Yakov Bok is a man accused of ritual murder; persecution drives him to triumph, demonstrating moral superiority over his accusers.

Yossarian—Lippy Yossarian is too smart to die, but not smart enough to evade his predicament in Joseph Heller's *Catch-22* (1961).

Yury—Boris Pasternak's *Doctor Zhivago* (1957) portrays anti-Marxist poet Yury Zhivago as a creative intellectual against the tumultuous background of revolutionary Russia.

Zooey—Best-looking of the Glass kids, Zooey spends time propping up his sister in J. D. Salinger's *Franny and Zooey* (1961).

Zorba—This uninhibited Greek bon vivant brings out the passion in those around him in Nikos Kazantzakis' *Zorba the Greek* (1946).

BIBLIOGRAPHY

Amazon.com.

Chernow, Barbara A. and George A. Vallasi, eds. *The Columbia Encyclopedia*. Columbia University Press and Houghton Mifflin, 1975.

Cohen, Carol, ed. *Benet's Reader's Encyclopedia*, 3rd edition. New York: Harper & Row, 1987.

Drabble, Margaret, ed. *The Oxford Companion to English Literature*. Oxford: Oxford University Press, 1985.

Graves, Robert. *The Greek Myths*. New York: Penguin, 1955.

Hardwick, Michael and Mollie. *The Charles Dickens Companion*. New York: Holt, Rinehart and Winston, 1965.

Lieder, P. R., R. M. Lovett and R. K. Root, eds. *British Poetry and Prose*. Boston: Houghton Mifflin, 1951.

Magill, Frank N., ed. *Cyclopedia of Literary Characters*. New York: Harper & Row, 1963.

Microsoft Encarta. Funk & Wagnall's Corporation, 1994.

Seymour-Smith, Martin. *Dictionary of Fictional Characters*. New York: The Writer, Inc., 1992.

SparkNotes.com.

Steinbrummer, Chris and Otto Penzler. *Encyclopedia of Mystery and Detection*. New York: McGraw-Hill, 1976.

Wright, ed. *The Cambridge Edition Text: The Complete Works of William Shakespeare*. New York: Garden City Books, 1936.

INDEX